KU-592-107

AT the Sign of the *Fiſh*, in the Lower End of *Black-Horſe-Alley*, at the Steps near *Fleet-Bridge*; Liveth *William Browne*, who Maketh all Sorts of Fiſhing-Rods, Artificial Flyes, and Selleth *Kerbie*'s Hooks, the *Indian*-Weed, commonly called Graſs-Worm; Gentles, and all other Sorts of Fiſhing-Tackle.

Peter De la Fontaine GOLDSMITH
At the Golden Cup in Litchfield Street
SOHO. Makes, & Sells all Sorts of Gold & Silver
Plate, Swords, Rings, Jewells &c, at ȳ lowest prices

W. Hogarth f.

LONDON
TRADESMEN'S CARDS
OF THE XVIII CENTURY

AN ACCOUNT OF THEIR ORIGIN AND USE

BY

AMBROSE HEAL

NEW YORK
DOVER PUBLICATIONS, INC.

659·137

HERTFORDSHIRE
COUNTY LIBRARY
745·2

5333007
200/1071

C 6087389-2

Published in Canada by General Publishing Company, Ltd.,
30 Lesmill Road, Don Mills, Toronto, Ontario.

Published in the United Kingdom by Constable and Company,
Ltd., 10 Orange Street, London WC 2.

This Dover edition, first published in 1968,
is an unabridged and unaltered republication of the work
originally published by B. T. Batsford, Ltd., in 1925.

Library of Congress Catalog Card Number: 67-19613

Manufactured in the United States of America
Dover Publications, Inc.
180 Varick Street
New York, N. Y. 10014

PREFACE

IT is perhaps remarkable that no book has hitherto been published dealing with Tradesmen's Cards. That they appeal to collectors is evidenced by the attention paid to examples which happen to come up for sale in the Auction Rooms; and that they have interest and charm for those with antiquarian tastes—or, indeed, any æsthetic tastes at all—is apparent when a portfolio of them is shown.

Not only has no book ever been published on the subject, but references in archæological journals and collectors' magazines are of the scantiest nature and hard to track. The would-be student of these engravings has little or no information to help him when gauging the possibilities that a collection of this nature might afford.

It is with the intention, therefore, of making known the interests that are to be found in these Cards, and the hope that some information on the origins and uses of them may be useful, that this book has been compiled. To those who are already collectors, many of wider knowledge and more experience than mine, I cannot hope to bring much of interest. From these who know how wide the range of the subject is, I hope I may claim indulgence for any omissions in my selection of examples. To represent adequately all the varieties of types and the immense number of trades within the compass of a single volume is well-nigh impossible.

To the courteous officials of the Print Room and Library at the British Museum and the Victoria and Albert Museum I owe much help, and I gladly acknowledge all the ready assistance I have received from the Librarians of the Guildhall, the Bishopsgate Institute, and many other London libraries.

The kindness of the Countess of Mayo has allowed me frequent access to the collections of the late Hon. Gerald Ponsonby; and many others, notably Lord Winterton, Dr. Philip Norman, Mr. Paul de Castro, Mr. E. Beresford Chancellor, Mr. John Charrington, Mr. D. Citroen, Mr. Arthur Hill, and Mr. Howard Levis, have given me valuable information.

The notes on Heraldry and Costume are the work of E. F. D. H., whose erudition on these and most other subjects connected with the work has been continually under contribution.

The instigator of the book was Mr. A. J. A. Symons, Director of the First Edition Club, to whose relentless insistence its appearance is largely due; to him, also, I owe grateful acknowledgements for reading the proofs. It is, however, mainly the enthusiastic collaboration of Messrs. Batsford and the nucleus collection of plates got together some years before the war by the late Mr. Herbert Batsford and Mr. Percy J. Smith that have made the publication of the book in its present ample form at all possible.

Beaconsfield, April, 1925.   A. H.

CONTENTS

Jeane Tempell. Chimbley:
:Swepers at the Signe of the woman :
: Chimbley Sweper in Nutners street
near the watch house in Holborn

THIS EDITION BOUND and DISTRIBUT

BY REMPLOY LTD

CHAPTER I

THE PURPOSES AND INTERESTS OF TRADESMEN'S CARDS

TRADESMEN'S CARDS—or the shorter form, 'Trade Cards'—is the term in most general use for the engravings which form the subject of this monograph. It is not altogether a satisfactory term, and when applied to the early examples it is an inaccurate one, for these were not confined to the use of tradesmen, nor were they of pasteboard.

It is, however, better than the alternatives, 'Tradesmen's Bills' or 'Shopkeepers' Bills,' although the latter was the one used by the eighteenth-century tradesman himself, for we find the printers who supplied them called themselves 'Engravers of Shopkeepers' Bills.' It has not seemed expedient to revive this form, for they were used not solely by shopkeepers and for other purposes than for accounts. Nor does 'Tradesmen's Bills' commend itself. Strictly, the word 'bill' has the sense of a placard or advertisement, but more generally bears less pleasant associations which might deter the collector.

'Tradesmen's Cards,' therefore, best meets the case, despite the fact that they were not cards, but sheets of paper ranging up to folio size. This is the term, moreover, sanctioned and now invariably used by those erudite gentlemen who compile the Book Sales catalogues and whose profound knowledge is at once the admiration and despair of those who indulge in this insidious and delectable form of reading. The tradesman's card with which we are familiar to-day is actually a card, and it is the impoverished descendant of the noble and distinguished-looking sheets which were in common use up till a hundred years ago. The reinforced variety on pasteboard was not generally adopted until the Victorian era, though I have seen one or two examples as early as 1780.

The exact purpose of the Trade Card is not generally agreed upon. Some say that it was primarily as an account, and that it was frequently used for this purpose cannot be denied, for in many of the examples here shown the back of the Bill has been utilized in this way, and in many other instances, where space has permitted, the front of it has been so used also. That this was not its principal function I think is fairly conclusively shown by the fact that we find Tradesmen using the ordinary invoice heading for their accounts, and at the same time using the more ornate form of Trade Card for announcement purposes. Or, alternatively, one side will take the more elaborate form of the Trade Card, announcing a name and address, and setting forth a list of wares, while on the back of this will be a less decorative billheading starting off with the words 'Bought of' and with ample space provided for the items of the account. Of these double-faced forms the one shown on Plate No. XLI. of Matthew Pearson, Haberdasher at the *Royal Point* in Tavistock Street, Covent Garden, is a good example. The illustration shows the more decorative and informing side, but on the back of this is a condensed billhead with an account made out in the name of Mrs. Garrick for lengths of dress material—'Shaneal' (Chenille), 'Taffety,' 'White Sattin,' and so forth. This account is dated 1774, two years previous to David Garrick's last appearance on the stage.

As I have mentioned, there are numerous examples where the Trade Bill has been used for short accounts or for giving memoranda of prices, but when these occur on the face, it is only where the blank space provides an opportunity. At other times the back of the Bill is used for this purpose. More usually, and in all the best examples, the engraving giving the Trader's name, his sign and his address, and the setting forth of the list of his wares occupies the whole of the face of the Bill, except for the well-proportioned margins which are an integral part of the design of all carefully planned pages. This announcement, then, of his shop is the first and principal use of the Tradesman's Card, and much skill has gone to the making of it.

Numerous as the examples are which have been used for the purpose of accounts, by far the majority found in public and private collections have no writing on them at all, and in selecting examples for this book I have, whenever possible, given only those Cards which are not defaced by accounts. Where accounts occur on the backs of specimens I have not necessarily rejected them, for the accounts are often extremely interesting in themselves, giving the descriptions and the prices of goods, and fixing the dates when these forms were actually used.

It is not always easy to assign accurate dates to Tradesmen's Cards, for although they bear indications of their period, the same form lingered on for many years. The name of a firm does not necessarily change on the death of its proprietor, nor the Sovereign's head on the Sign at the death of the reigning monarch. Queen Anne,

though dead, still persisted on Trade Cards of the reign of George the
Third. I have in my collection one delightful example of the un-
daunted spirit long endeared to us by 'The Vicar of Bray.' This
particular specimen emanated from a well-known firm of Blacking
Manufacturers whose name is a household word and whose admirable
product is happily still with us. The legend on this egregiously
economical Billhead runs thus:

'SO AND SO, SO AND SO AND CO.

BLACKING MANUFACTURERS TO   MAJESTY'

No turn in the affairs of State found this astute manufacturer of
boot polish unprovided for—he just filled in the accommodating
blank, 'His' or 'Her' as the case demanded, and went on gaily
making blacking.

Sometimes the Cards were called ' Shop-bills or Message-cards,' but
of their use as communications I have found no actual examples
—merely contemporary references to the term.

I have gone into this question of the right or primary use of the
Tradesman's Card rather fully, as it is apt to be misconceived, and the
distinction between the Trade Card and the Billhead is not always
easy to draw, but at least we may be sure that, however ornate and
elaborate the form may be, if it contains the words 'Bought of . . . .'
then we may know that it is a Billhead and no true Trade Card.

So far, then, I have tried to define the term Trade Card, to justify
the use of that term in preference to other names for it, and to describe
its uses. I propose now to put forward some reasons why the Trade
Card has an interest for any of us, and what is its particular interest for
the collector.

I fully realize that the Tradesman's Card is an advertisement.
I have tried to show that its primary use is that of an advertisement.
I make no higher claim for it than that, though I realize that the uses of
advertisement are not sweet to all. Many of these uses and methods—
one need not particularize further—are distasteful in the extreme.
But the old time tradesman's card is a straightforward announcement
of his wares: it tells you where they are to be found, it gives his name,
the sign of his shop, or his number in the street. It does this without
palaver, without unseemly parade, and without pretence that it is
either a sermon or a novelette. It does it in a seemly way, often in a
very decorative and interesting way. It avoids those errors against

good taste into which some of our modern advertisers are so easily beguiled. The lettering in the early examples is almost uniformly of a high standard of achievement; the design, or, as advertising men say, 'the layout,' is dignified and well spaced, the ornament well drawn and the copper-plate engraving is highly accomplished.

To anyone with a liking for old things the Trade Card must make an irresistible appeal. It is so convincingly of its own time. There is no affectation of the pseudo-antique, nor does it attempt to be cleverly up to date. It is the plain statement of the shopkeeper or merchant to his customer. It has the quaintness of its period, the characteristic phrasing, the picturesque quality of the old world wares, described by fine resonant names: Grograms, Padusoys, Callimancoes, Lutestrings, Prunellas and the like, long since fallen into disuse, but everyday words of their time.

The old Signs that hung over the shop doors and are reproduced on the Traders' Cards are of great antiquity and interest. The names of the old streets, many of which have long since been swept away, such as 'Knaves' Acre,' 'Rosemary Lane,' 'Wendegaynlane,' take one's imagination quite apart from their historical or topographical connections.

In those cases where an account is made out on the back there is the interest of comparing the prices of those days with our own.

To come across an item like

> '15½ yds Blue and White Clouded and Flower'd Lustring at 7/- a yard.'

or one that appears in another of Mrs. Garrick's bills rendered by Jeremiah Hawkes, Mercer at *The Wheatsheaf* in Tavistock Street, which reads

> '18 yds Pompadour strip'd and figured Sattin at 6/- a yard.'

is to be brought face to face with something which combines the quality of a romance and the excitement of a bargain sale.

Apart from the archæological interests mentioned, Tradesmen's Cards provide various records. The earlier examples, comprising the Sign of the house or a City Company, have distinct heraldic value. The later ones, wherein street scenes are frequently met with, illustrate architecture and costume. To the student of commerce they are first-hand evidence of markets and prices, to the artist they have a quality and a technique which is worth consideration.

The collecting of these little engravings has a peculiar fascination. It leads along one of those pleasant, sequestered bypaths of that curiously detached country known only to collectors. One of its chief attractions is that it is so little frequented. To the man who likes to regard his collection as an investment, this form of collecting affords no opportunities—a display of his portfolios will fail to create any great impression on the bulk of his acquaintances. There are no highly sensational finds such as provide meat and drink to the collector of early editions—no First Folio in the 'Tuppenny Box.' To those who can deny themselves these fierce delights, to those who can afford to spend a little money and a good deal of patience on the pursuit—to the humble but keen collector—the Trade Card presents advantages which the better known branches of the collectors' art do not enjoy.

There are, of course, the disadvantages of this quality of modesty. The object of your search can elude you in a tantalizing way. Frequently you go into what looks like a promising little print shop, and the proprietor will not have heard of such a thing as a Trade Card. He regards you with polite tolerance mingled with suspicion. He wishes to give you the impression that he is more familiar with the term Art than that of Trade. The name does not command his respect. He allows you to leave his shop with little show of regret at your short stay. At the larger and better known print dealers you will find little enthusiasm for so humble a commodity, except in a few of the more discriminating shops. I find the simplest way is to carry a few specimens in my pocket in order to save explanations.

Nor will the salerooms prove more productive. You will search the fascinating catalogues of those haunts of wealthy collectors in Bond Street or Leicester Square for months on end without lighting on a single lot. Now and again, it is true, private collections will come under the hammer, all beautifully mounted on thick cards and carefully tabulated under the headings of various trades, or according to their topographical interests, but these are rare and wonderful days.

To the collector who is of the aristocracy, he who buys Early Manuscripts, Incunabula, Ming China, Enamels, Ivories, Italian Primitives, Waterford Glass and the like, to him come post haste the sumptuously illustrated catalogues, and at his stupendous bidding the voices of the crowd at Christie's sink to a respectful hush.

Not so, but far otherwise, is the way of the Trade Card Collector. His quiet path lies alongside that of the diligent seeker after the lesser known antiquities. He is the man, for example, who patiently puts together print by print, cutting by cutting, the history of some small lovable village now engulfed in Greater Suburbdom. Or he, again, it is, who confines his passion to the less sought after *rariora,* such as Fire Insurance plates, the old brasses from horse trappings, the small wares turned in wood, 'coloured juveniles,' or perhaps in lighter moments—valentines.

For the likes of him are the little shops in the by-streets, or in the small country town. A sharp eye and an indefatigable spirit of the chase are needed by the picker-up of these less considered trifles. With these, and on his own chosen ground, he can hold his own with the rich man, nor are the snares of the unprincipled dealer laid for such quiet folk. His modest way is untroubled by the wiles of the professional faker or the ingenious 'restorer.' It is worth nobody's while to produce elaborate fakes of such simple things. True there are a few reprints of cards which have been engraved by, or attributed to, Hogarth (see p. 63), but these are aimed at another and more wealthy class of amateur, and will not often beguile the true collector of Trade Cards, whose concern is not primarily with celebrated artists and such like, but with the old shopkeeper and his quaint wares, or his old street.

Indeed, it is just because people have failed to set store by these modest sheets, it is precisely because they were such common affairs of everyday life, that they have not been preserved. Old boxes of bills, put aside perhaps for generations and forgotten a hundred years ago, now and again come to light; in the pattern-books of dead and gone engravers, in old scrap-books and other odd hiding places unsuspected stores of Trade Cards may be hidden.

It is curiously aloof and detached, this by-way of collecting. It is not bound up with any notabilities in history or literature or the stage. Even the most proficient Trade Card engravers, such as Bickham, Cole, Fourdrinier, and Wilkes are known only to the few. In this respect it is unlike the somewhat similar, but much more popular quest of the Bookplate collector or that of those rarer birds, the collectors of Invitation Tickets, Tickets for Theatrical Benefits, Pleasure Gardens and Fêtes, and those for Lotteries or for Funerals; though to this group our collector of Trade Bills is most nearly akin.

In all this it may be said that I have only put forward a very negative claim for the interest of my subject, yet within its limits it has a very definite call on the consideration of those who have a concern for the Customs and Fashions of the past two hundred years. As records of the old streets, the signs of the old traders, and the descriptions of their wares, these Cards give the closest indications. Some, too, as I said, afford intimate glimpses of the architecture and costume of their times.

For their æsthetic qualities, those of the eighteenth century are far in advance of our equivalents of to-day. The lettering is invariably well drawn and well spaced, and the designing of the devices, if sometimes crude, is always direct and interesting. They reflect the art of the engraver through two centuries.

Though essentially a humble instrument of either advertisement or invoice—or both—the Tradesman's Card is a source of wide archæological interest. It is just because of its common workaday purpose that its value as a record is so true, and this it is that gives it a touch of vitality that many volumes of historical research do not possess.

There is about these old prints an attractive something which many an old shop has: a delightful air of quaintness that is irresistible. They carry with them the prosaic, uneventful day-to-day history of their trade, the changes in Fashion—themselves the reflection of the influences of a wider world—the development or decay of an industry. In their way they have a touch of romance. Not, perhaps, the Romance of Commerce as we have it described to us in our own, and more particularly in American magazines, but the plain tale of the shop-keeper, proud enough of his trade and his distinctive device to have his advertisement sheets well designed, beautifully lettered and finely engraved.

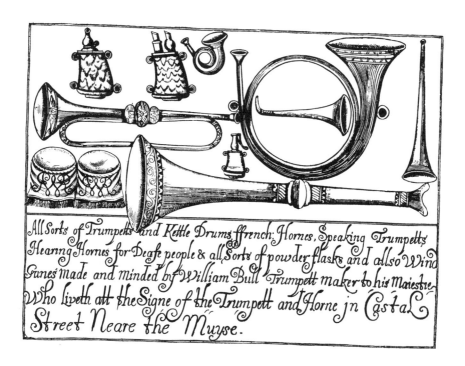

All Sorts of Trumpetts and Kettle Drums ffrench: Hornes, Speaking Trumpetts, Hearing Hornes for Deafe people & all Sorts of powder flasks and allso Wind Gunes made and minded by William Bull Trumpett maker to his Maiestie, Who liveth att the Signe of the Trumpett and Horne in Castal Street Neare the Muyse.

CHAPTER II

HISTORY AND DEVELOPMENT

JUDGING from the scarcity of examples which can be definitely assigned to the seventeenth century, we may assume that the Tradesman's Card had hardly come into general use before the beginning of the eighteenth century. Specimens dating from 1700 to 1720 are also exceedingly rare, and a careful search through many collections has failed to produce more than a few score which can be definitely so dated. Others might be assumed, judging from their general character, to be as early, but where evidence as to date has not been traceable I have preferred to omit definite mention. It may be premised of these very early cards that many of them are either those we should now class as belonging to the professions or to those trades which, generally speaking, served the more educated classes: Arms-painters, Auctioneers, Booksellers, Makers of Scientific Instruments, Moneylenders, Opticians, Surgeons, and Writing Masters are those mostly met with. At that time the printed word was still little understood by the common folk, and this naturally restricted the use of the Trade Card to a limited circle.

That which is believed to be the earliest English Trade Card known is in the form of a plain type-printed sheet, and runs as follows:

> Whosoever shall desire to purchase or put to Sale . . . through the want of present money May eyther in their owne names, or in the name of any other trusted by them, have secure means with all Priuacy requisite; for the speedy effecting what shall be desired.
>
> At the Porcht-house against St. *Andrewe's* Church in Holborne London.
> God save our gracious King *Charles*.

This strikes a note familiarised to us by the alluring letters which so often brighten our breakfast tables to-day, but we sadly miss the sonorous old English names which commonly grace these helpful offers to the temporarily embarrassed. Indeed, the stark anonymity of this one casts an air of suspicion which the sanctity of the 'Porcht House against St. Andrewe's Church' barely dispels. The date of this Card cannot be later than 1630, for six copies of it were found bound as end papers into a book which was published in that year. Of these, however, two copies were very defective. There are, therefore, only four perfect ones known, of which one was sold when

Mr. J. E. Hodgkin's Collection came under the hammer at Sotheby's in 1914. Another extremely rare example occurred in the same sale: that of William Thorpp, bookseller, dated 1664, and of this it was said that only one other impression was known to exist. Below the Sign of *The Hand and Bible* runs the inscription—

> 'Printed for William Thorpp Bookseller in the City of Chester and are to be sould by him there at his shop *at the Hand and Bible* neere the high Crosse and at *the Stationers Armes* in the Watergate Street where alsoe Books both new and Old are to bee bound and sold.'

The very earliest Trade Card that I have in my own collection is that of Sylvanus Morgan, issued in the Sixteen Sixties just about the time of the publication of his *Sphere of Gentry*, which came out in 1661. The engraving of the Sign of *William Camden's Head* is taken from Gaywood's portrait. The text reads:

> 'Sylvanus Morgan is now returned to his former howse at the Northeast corner of the Royal Exchange *at the sign of the Camden's Head and City's Armes* where you may have Armes, Pedegrees, Funeral Escoutcheons, Ensignes Cornetts, Drums, Trumpett Banners or anything drawne according to Heraldry, also Palls of Velvit.'

Another early example is that of Henry Gyles, a Glass Painter, and the date of it is probably about ten years later than that of his brother artist, Sylvanus Morgan, about 1670.

Henry Gyles' Card has the distinction of being a Mezzotint engraving, possibly the only Trade Card for which this process was used. Searchers after rare Trade Cards at the British Museum will not find this example under that heading: it is classed under Mezzotint Portraits by Francis Place. The inscription reads:

> 'Glass Painting for windows, as Armes, Sundyals, History, Landskipt etc. Done by Henry Gyles of the City of York.'

In Chaloner Smith's *British Mezzotinto Portraits* this work is described in detail, and Thoresby mentions that the print was 'wrought in mezzotinto, when that art was known to few others, by the celebrated Mr. Francis Place.'

Henry Gyles resided at York, 1640-1700, and founded a school of glass painters there. In 1687 he painted a window at University College, Oxford.

In the Hodgkin Sale was a curious Broadside, said to be unique,

of *The King's* [James II] *Bagnio in Long Acre,* with an engraving of the
Bath, and giving its dimensions, charges, etc. This was dated 1686.

A small, but particularly representative, collection of Trade Cards of
the latter half of the seventeenth century is to be found in the two
large volumes devoted to London topographical prints, maps, etc., in
the Pepysian Library at Magdalene College, Cambridge. Amongst these
forty cards are four very interesting ones of Cutlers:—John Best 'at y*e*
Mace y*e* corner of Lumbard Street next y*e* Stocks Market,' Thomas
Bickerstaff 'liveing at the Signe of *y*e* Halberd* in Princes Streete,' John
Cooke, at the Signe of *The Shears* in little Lombard Street, and
Nicholas Croucher at *y*e* Flaming Sword* in S*t* Paul's Churchyard. The
card that bears the earliest date in this collection is that of 'John Short
Wollen-Draper at the Signe of *The Black-Swan and Parrat* in Cannon
Streete.' On it are the arms of the Merchant Taylors Company and
the date 1654.

Two other rare Cards are mentioned by J. E. Hodgkin in his
Rariora, both by William Hogarth. One is that of James Figg, prize-
fighter, which, according to Ireland in his *Hogarth Illustrated,* had
then fetched as much as £8 8s.; the other is that of Peter de la Fontaine, goldsmith, which forms the frontispiece of this book.

A decorative class of Trade Card is the woodcut of the first half of
the eighteenth century. A very early example, which is to be found in
the Bagford Collection at the British Museum, is that depicting a Calico
Printer at work, with his small assistant colouring his blocks. Green's
History of the English People attributes this to the reign of James II.
(See Plate IX.)

Two other typical woodcuts are illustrated on Plates XVIII and
LXXVII.

We now come to the palmy days of the Trade Card, from 1720
to 1770. This period stands out, not only on account of the high
excellence of the engraving, but also because of the interest attaching
to the Traders' Signs, rendered in a highly decorative manner by the
accomplished 'Engravers of Shop Bills,' as they called themselves.

It is interesting at this point to note the development in motive.
To begin with, we find that the important feature is the Sign, more
or less heraldically treated, and below it a simple panel of well-drawn
lettering. Of this group the following are the most typical examples:
Plates Nos. III, IV, XXVIII, XLIII, LV, LVII, LXII, LXV,
XCV.

In the second stage the Traders' Sign is still the predominant feature, but instead of the severely simple treatment it is now enclosed in an ornamental frame characteristically shown in

Plates Nos. XVII, XIX, XXI, XXXVII, XLIV, XLVII, LVI, LXXXVI, XCI, C.

At the third development the Sign is still retained, but yields pride of place to the representation of wares which figure prominently in the design of the ornamental frame, as reference to the following Plates will show:

Frontispiece, I, XXXVIII, XLVI, XLVIII, LXX, LXXX, LXXXI.

In many of these plates the influences of Thomas Chippendale and the vogue for chinoiseries are plainly manifest.

An alternative was to reduce the Sign to a still more subservient position and devote the main interest of the design to a rather elaborate and symbolic representation of the trade, as in—

Plate No. XI.   Richard Siddall, Chymist *at the Golden Head,* in Panton Street.

Plate No. XLIX.   Mrs. Holt's Italian Warehouse *at ye Two Olive Posts* in ye Broad Part of the Strand.

and Plate No. LXXII of Richard Warren the Perfumer *at the Golden Fleece* in Mary le Bonne Street.

Next we come to the period when the Sign has disappeared altogether, and the interest is entirely confined to the display of goods. The numbering of the houses has not yet been adopted on the Cards, but instead of the Sign we get a descriptive form of address, such as occurs on the card of—

Richard Severn, Jeweller & Toyman, the Corner of Paul's-Grave-Head-Court near Temple Barr, London.

Here we find the fashion of the Trade Card necessarily following on the enforced abolition of the old hanging Signs in 1762, when the numbering of the houses began to take its place.   This transition is shown in the following:

Plates Nos. XXIV, XXXIII, LXXIII, XCIII.

A very favourite variant of this method of supplanting the old Sign with conventional designs embodying the wares of the shop was to introduce a scene giving a pictorial representation of the trade being carried on, as in Plates Nos. XXXIV, LII, LIII, LXVII, LXVIII, LXIX, LXXVII.

This style of design was a very favourite one of William Hogarth, a list of whose Trade Cards will be found on p 63.

The last development which is covered by the period dealt with in this book is that wherein street numbering has begun to be adopted generally, and a classic form of decoration, reflecting the prevalent style of ornament brought into fashion by the brothers Adam, is the characteristic feature.

J. Seago, Printseller and Bookseller, High Street, St. Giles', near Tottenham Court Road, was probably something in the nature of a 'last ditcher,' and stood out against the new-fangled notion of numbering. He was not, however, entirely unswayed by the movement towards a new elegance, for the graceful design shown on Plate II is a distinct advance on his former Card, which gives a very unprepossessing portrait of an uncouth looking old ruffian labelled 'Old Simon,' a notorious character in St. Giles' about 1780. These latter-day refinements, both of design and orderliness, are represented in:

Plate No. II. Seago, Printseller, High Street, St. Giles'.

Plate No. XXVI. Law, Dentist, 10 St. Albans Street, Pall Mall.

and Plate No. XXXII. Ross, Frame-maker, 113 Gt. Portland Street.

With the beginning of the nineteenth century the design of the Trade Card began to deteriorate sadly. The lettering still retained a great deal of the old charm, but the tradition soon got overlaid by the affectations of the Victorian era. These later Cards, however, though lacking in distinction, still have a quaint interest of their own time.

CHAPTER III

SHOP SIGNS AND THE TRADESMEN'S CARDS

THE CONNECTION between the old Shop Sign and the Trade Card is necessarily a very close one. It has been seen in the previous chapter how the Trade Card began by being a simple rendering of the Shop Sign, and how as these Signs fell into disuse it gradually became elaborated and ornamented with the representations of the shop-keeper's wares, and finally how, when the street numbering became firmly established, the Sign itself was altogether ousted.

It is interesting, therefore, to look into the history of signboards, and anyone who wishes to study this fascinating subject should read Larwood and Hotten's *History of Signboards*, 1866, and Mr. Philip Norman's *London Signs and Inscriptions,* though this latter refers more particularly to sculptured Signs. The late Mr. F. G. Hilton Price did a great deal of valuable research work in this direction, much of which will be found in the *Records of the London Topographical Society*, Vols. II, III, IV, and V, as well as in his own books, *The Signs of Old Lombard Street, The Signs of Old Fleet Street,* and the articles which appeared in the *Middlesex and Hertfordshire Notes and Queries,* on the Signs of the old houses in the Strand in the seventeenth and eighteenth centuries. With the assistance of these authorities I have made the following quite elementary notes.

The Egyptians seemed to have made occasional use of inscriptions to draw attention to the whereabouts of a trade. Whether the Greek Signs were carved or painted or merely displayed the natural object, is uncertain from the references made by Aristotle. The more general practice of the Romans, as we may still see at Pompeii, was a panel in relief beside the shop front. The earliest forms were some simple object typical of the trade—a hand for the glover, a bunch of grapes for the vintner. In the Middle Ages coats-of-arms, crests and badges began to be used, for as particular trades were confined to particular streets the trader felt the need for some more individual and distinctive Sign. Sometimes the shopkeeper's own name would suggest a rebus, as Robert Legg Upholsterer *at the Sign of ye Leg* in Holborn (compare Plate No. XCIX).

After the Great Fire it became more common to have the Sign carved on a stone panel and let into the face of the building, but the old hanging Signs were either fixed to the front of the house or to a post standing in front of it; in both cases the supporting ironwork was used as a decorative feature. When these supports became dilapidated they were a source of danger to the wayfarer, and public opinion called for their dismissal. Most people could by then read sufficiently well to decipher a name or a number, so a more convenient method was wanted. The removal of the Signs was proclaimed, and in 1762 they began to be cleared away, and the numbering of the Streets to be instituted. Previous to this, however, Great Prescott Street, in Goodman's Fields, had, in 1708, led the way to the innovation by numbering the houses after the manner of the staircases in the Inns of Court and Chancery. The last Streets to keep their Signs hanging were Wood Street and Whitecross Street, where they remained till 1773.*

In the history of Trade Cards this period is an all-important one, as the presence or absence of the number of the house will help us to determine the date of the Card. For many years the Sign continued to be used on the Tradesman's Card as the mark of the house, supplementing the numbers, and in many Cards the transition may be noted, the number being spatchcocked into the old copper-plate.

The art of the sign-painter had its headquarters in Harp Alley, Shoe Lane, though besides the ordinary practitioner many famous artists were induced to turn their hands to sign-painting. Of these, Clarkson is known to have painted the *Shakespeare's Head*, in Little Russell Street, Drury Lane, for which he is said to have received £500. Others were John Baker (one of the original R.A.'s); Charles Catton, R.A., who did one for Wright, the famous coachmaker in Long Acre; Cipriani, also an R.A.; Samuel Wale, R.A., and the marine painter, Smirke, R.A. Hogarth and Morland both painted Signs, and that by David Cox at the *Royal Oak* at Bettws-y-Coed is still well known to visitors. Just recently there have been slight evidences of a revival in this ancient craft, and one or two of our decorative painters have produced some good signboards.

It will strike many that there frequently occurs a curious lack of connection between the Sign and the trade carried on under it.

*Wheatley, in his *London Past and Present*, referring to a house, on the site of which now stands part of the Grand Hotel, quotes the following statement from Smith's *Nollekens:* 'This house was No. 1 Strand and was the first house in London that was numbered.'

Addison, writing to *The Spectator,* says: 'I would enjoin every shop-keeper to make use of a sign which bears some affinity to the wares in which he deals. A cook should not live at *The Boot* nor a shoe-maker at the *Roasted Pig.*' Such incongruity was often accounted for by the fact that when one tradesman succeeded to a shop where a different trade had been carried on he retained the old Sign, if it was a well-known one, and a landmark in the district. Or again, if he wished to retain the old Sign, for this or some other reason, and at the same time felt the necessity of having one which was appropriate to his own calling, he would not scruple to combine the two symbols. Occasionally this was done with rather incongruous results, as in the case of *The Three Nuns and a Hare, The Lamb and Dolphin, The Bull and Bedpost.* It was quite common, too, for a young tradesman starting on his own account to add to his own Sign that of the master whom he had served. Other combinations, which on the face of them do not seem to have any particular connection, are the result of corruption, as in the case of the famous old London coaching inn, *The Bull and Mouth,* which is generally supposed to have come from Boulogne Mouth—the entrance to Boulogne Harbour, that town having been taken by Henry VIII; though another theory that it might have originally been the Bowl and Mouth seems less far-fetched. Some again were, no doubt, the outcome of lack of understanding; for example, in the case of *The Leg and Star,* this was possibly nothing else than the two insignia of the Order of the Garter—the garter being appropriately represented on the leg. The *Leg and Seven Stars* is but the attempt of one tradesman to outshine another by annexing a larger constellation, though the Seven Stars of the Pleiades is a well-known Masonic emblem. One publican near Bristol went the length of putting up *The Fourteen Stars.*

Curious Signs are such as *The Red M. and Dagger, The Pistol and L., The Pistol and C.*; the initial being that of the shopkeeper's name, or that of one of his predecessors. A reference is made in Larwood and Hotten to these Signs: 'The Sign (that of *The Red M. and Dagger*) occurs among the Bagford Bills; there is a similar one amongst the Banks Bills—*The Pistol and C.,* the sign of John Crook, a razor maker in the Great Turnstile, Holborn, *circa* 1787; the bill represents a renaissance scutcheon with a pistol, above it a C and surgical instruments disseminated on the field.' Compare Plate No. LXXXI. A similar Sign appears on the Trade Card of Edward

Tymperon, razor maker at *The E.T. and Crown* in Russell Street, Drury Lane.

But the study of the Signboard is an immense subject in itself, and can only be slightly touched on here in connection with its bearing on the Trade Card. Another offshoot of the Signboard is the Tradesman's Token, a subject which has fascinated many collectors and on which much has been written. To collectors of London Tokens, J. H. Burns' book on the Beaufoy Collection is well known; this and Akerman's *Tradesmen's Tokens* will be found useful to the searchers after old Signs.

At the time of the coronation of King Edward VII the great bankers and insurance companies of Lombard Street met together and decided that the most appropriate form of street decoration they could contribute to the occasion was to revive the old Signs belonging to their street. This suggestion was adopted by twenty-three of the companies and a unique and interesting scheme of street decoration was the result. Unhappily only seven of these have been allowed to remain. Of Signs still to be seen in our streets a few examples persist— the Barber's Pole and the Three Golden Balls (originally Three Blue Balls) of the pawnbrokers are those most frequently met with. Other devices occasionally seen are the Arm and Hammer of the gold-beater, the Kettle and the Hat which hang in front of ironmongers' and hatters' shops, the Fishing Rod and Dangling Trout over the fishing tackle shops, the Roll of Tobacco and the Highlander outside the tobacconists'. These and a few still rarer signs are all that remain. In the last few years there have been encouraging signs of a revival of the art of the sign-painter, and a concerted effort, were it made by the tradesmen, might well lead to an added gaiety in our streets. Indeed, the work of many of our modern artists is well suited to the symbolic treatment of shop signs, and there are many designers quite capable of producing most interesting decorations if our traders would provide the opportunities.

CHAPTER IV

ARMS, EFFIGIES, AND OTHER EMBLEMS IN TRADESMEN'S CARDS

ROYAL ARMS

Where the Royal Arms are displayed on the Tradesman's Card we get an indication of its date. Thus where we have a shield showing in the

1st Grand Quarter, England and France quarterly
2nd „ „ Scotland
3rd „ „ Ireland
4th „ „ England and France quarterly

the date is confined to the reigns of the Stuart Kings, 1603-1689.

With the accession of William and Mary in 1689 the Stuart arms were differenced with the arms of Nassau.

In 1702, when Queen Anne came to the throne, there was a reversion to the Stuart arms until the Union with Scotland in 1707, after which date we get:

1st and 4th Grand Quarters. England impaling Scotland.
2nd „ „ France.
3rd „ „ Ireland.

On the advent of the House of Hanover, George I, 1714, we get a change in the 4th Grand Quarter which, instead of repeating the 1st Grand Quarter, is now devoted to the arms of Hanover, but from January 1st, 1801, the arms of France disappeared, and we get quarterly:

1st and 4th England.
2nd Scotland.
3rd Ireland.

Over all, on an escutcheon of pretence, Hanover. These arms were borne from 1801 until 1837, when, on the accession to the throne of Queen Victoria, the arms of Hanover were removed.

Tradesmen's Cards bearing Royal Arms are shown on Plates Nos. V, VI, XII, XXVI, XXXIV, and XLVII.

ARMS OF COMPANIES, GUILDS, ETC.

The arms of the City of London are quite often displayed, usually in conjunction with those of the Company appropriate to the man's trade. Instances amongst the illustrations here given will be found in

> Plate No. III.   Thomas Pickett, 'Citizen and Brazier.'
> „ No. XVI. Casaltine and Mathews, Clothiers.

Arms of the City Guilds will be found in

> Plate No. X.   Carpenters' Company.
> „ No. LXXVII.   Pinmakers' Company.
> „ No. LXXXIX. Tallow Chandlers' Company.
> „ No. XCV.   Turners' Company.

Badges of the London Assurance, the Sun, and the Royal Exchange Fire Insurance Companies are introduced into the Card of John Bristow, engine maker (see Plate No. XXXI).

At 'Mrs. Holt's Italian warehouse at *ye Two Olive Posts* in ye Broad part of the Strand' (see Plate No. XLIX) are proudly displayed the arms of the Medici family, more, one imagines, by way of introducing a little local colour than by any prescriptive right.

ROYAL EFFIGIES

Effigies of Royal Personages are fairly frequently met with, and examples are found of most of the reigning monarchs and their consorts through nearly four centuries. An interesting one of Queen Elizabeth occurs on the Card of 'Thomas Paulin, mercer, at *The Statue of Queen Elizabeth* in Tavistock Street, Covent Garden,' engraved by Sherborne, and a notable Portrait Sign is reproduced on the beautifully engraved Card of 'Joseph Trigge, Mercer, *At the Sign of Queen Elizabeth's Head* within three doors of St. Paul's in Ludgate Street.' When this Sign was painted it attracted so much attention that *The Spectator,* January 8, 1743, said:

> 'The other day, going down Ludgate Street, several people were gaping at a very splendid sign of Queen Elizabeth which far excelled all the other signs in the street, the painter having shown a masterly judgment and the carver and gilder much pomp and splendour. It looked rather like a capital picture in a gallery than a sign in the Street.'

A comprehensive Sign is that which is given on the Card of 'Thomas Small, haberdasher, at the *Three Protestant Queens* in Cheapside,' dated 1727. This combines the effigies of Queens Elizabeth, Mary, and Anne.

On the Card of a Quack Doctor is to be seen a delightful incident in the life of George III, described thus:

> 'His Majesty on the Esplanade at Weymouth graciously accepting a Box of Chings Patent Worm Lozenges which was presented to him as a Patent Medicine.'

The King in tricorne hat, kneebreeches and sword complete—his benefactor kneels before him.

EFFIGIES OF SAINTS

Exceedingly few instances of Saints occur on Tradesmen's Cards, presumably owing to the fact that the Patron Saint had passed away with the Reformation before the day of the Trade Card. On the old Signboard they had been quite usual—St. Crispin for the Shoemakers, St. Martin for the Printers and Booksellers, St. Dunstan for the Goldsmiths. St. George was a general patron and the particular Saint of the metropolis. St. Peter and his Cross Keys were adopted by Locksmiths, St. Catherine with her Wheel was a charge in the Turners' Arms, and St. Lawrence's Gridiron in the Arms of the Girdlers' Company; this last saint also sanctified the Sign and Trade Card of the *Blossoms* Inn of Lawrence Lane, Cheapside. The emblems appropriate to the evangelists were, however, quite common on the Signboards—*The Eagle* of St. John, *The Lion* of St. Mark, *The Bull* of St. Luke, and *The Angel* of St. Matthew.

Among the few Saints that do figure on Trade Cards is one that occurs on a mid-eighteenth-century example issued from 'James Watson at his Scots Holland warehouse in Charles Street, Covent Garden,' where St. Andrew is portrayed though not proclaimed. On another Card the *Sign of St. Peter* is borne by a locksmith. A third Saint appears on a large and finely engraved Card in the time of George III, the text of which, rather curiously, is entirely in French. It is that of 'Thomas Moore, Marchand fabricant de Bas et Bonneterie de la Majesté Britanique demeurant *à l'Enseigne de l'Evesque Blaze* dans Chiswell Street.' The holy Bishop is portrayed holding a Bible in one hand and bearing in the other the emblem of his martyrdom—an iron comb. It is this instrument which connects him with the Wool-combers, whose Patron Saint he is. This interesting Card is reproduced on Plate No. XLVII, and it will be noticed that there are two some-what incongruous pendants to this Cappadocian Bishop of the first century—a 'bas de Soye' and a primitive type of umbrella.

POETS, ARTISTS, AND SCIENTISTS

Men of Letters adorn the Cards of many Booksellers: those met with are Chaucer, Ben Jonson, Dryden, Erasmus, Horace, Pope, Otway, Seneca, Shakespeare, and Virgil; and the Heads of Archimedes and Sir Isaac Newton appear on those of makers of scientific instruments, those of Glauber and of Paracelsus on chemists'. Hogarth's Head is displayed on the Card of John Smith, Map and Printseller of Cheap-side, drawn by C. Vanloo and engraved by Clowes, and also on the Card of Ryall and Withy, Booksellers and Printsellers at *The Hogarth Head and Dial,* Salisbury Court and Fleet Street. A portrait of the practitioner himself is given on Plate No. LXXXVIII of Charles Peter.

Another instance of the Portrait Card is that of Christopher Pinch-beck, Senr., clockmaker, who invented the copper and zinc alloy named after him. The Quack Doctor Eldridge too—'The Norwich Artist'—is a notable example in the Banks Collection.

On a very fine Card, dated 1717, appears a portrait of James Smith, Artificial Eye maker, by S. Tuncks, and engraved by J. Pine who himself kept a print shop in St. Martin's Lane and was a friend of Hogarth.

There is also a delightful portrait by R. Cooper, dated 1762, on the Card of 'William Bentley, Teacher of the Mathematicks, Kingston, Surrey.'

TRADE EMBLEMS

Many emblems were used indiscriminately, such as *The Red Lion, The Star,* and *The Crown.* On the other hand, certain trades adopt Signs peculiar to their particular craft. An attempt has been made to classify these, and a list is given of those symbols which are most generally used in the various trades, though it is by no means complete.

Trade	*Emblems employed*
Bakers	PLOUGH, ‖ WHEATSHEAF
Booksellers	ANGEL AND BIBLE, ‖ BIBLE, ‖ BIBLE AND DOVE
Braziers and Metal Trades	ANVIL AND BELLOWES
	CHAMBER GRATE
	BROWN TEA KETTLE AND LAMP
	DOG'S HEAD IN THE IRON POT
	FRYING PAN (see Plate III)
	GOLDEN EWER
	GRIDIRON
	HARROW. ‖ HARROW AND ANCHOR
	LOCK AND HINGE. ‖ ST. PETER AND KEY
	STOW GRATE
	TEA KETTLE
	THREE BELLS
	TRUMPET
	TWO CANDLESTICKS AND BELL
Breeches Makers	BOOT AND BREECHES (see Plate IV)
	BUCK AND BREECHES
Brush Makers	FOUR BRUSHES
Cabinet Makers, Carpenters, Upholsterers and Undertakers	ARMS OF CARPENTERS' COMPANY
	CHAIR AND TEA CHEST (see Plate VIII)
	FOUR COFFINS
	ROYAL BED
	'ROYAL TENT' AND 'THREE TENTS' (Arms of the Upholders' Company)
	THREE COVERED CHAIRS AND WALNUT TREE
Chemists	GLAUBER'S HEAD
Clockmakers	DIAL (see Plate XIV)
Clothiers and Slopmen	CHILD'S COAT
	JOLLY SAILOR (see Plate XVII)
	LAMB (see Plate XVI)

Trade	*Emblems employed*
Coalmen	OLD COLLIER AND CART (see Plate XVIII)
Confectioners	PINE APPLE (see Plate XX)
Cutlers	CASE OF KNIVES SAW AND CROWN (see Plate LXXX)
Dairymen	ASS AND FOAL (see Plate XXV)
Drapers, Mercers, Haberdashers, etc.	BLACKMOOR'S HEAD (see Plate LVI) COVENTRY CROSS GOLDEN FLEECE (see Plate CI) GOLDEN SHUTTLE HEN AND CHICKENS INDIAN KING (see Plate LXIII) INDIAN QUEEN (see Plate LXI) LAMB AND SPREAD EAGLE (see Plate LXIV) OLD BLACK BOY (see Plate LIV) ROYAL POINT (see Plate XLI) SPINNING WHEEL THREE ANGELS THREE NUNS AND WHEATSHEAF (see Plate LIX) TURK'S HEAD (see Plate LVIII) WHEATSHEAF (see Plate LV) WOOL PACK (see Plate C)
Dyers	GREEN MAN RAINBOW AND ANCHOR RAINBOW AND DOVE RAINBOW AND THREE PIDGONS (see Plate XXVIII)
Fishing Tackle Makers	DIAL AND FISH
Frame Makers, Carvers and Gilders	GOLDEN HEAD
Goldsmiths and Silversmiths	BOY AND CORAL (see Plate XXXVI) CROWN AND PEARL (see Plate XXXVII)

Trade	*Emblems employed*
Goldsmiths and Silversmiths (*contd.*)	GOLDEN ANGEL GOLDEN CUP (see Frontispiece) GOLDEN HAMMER RING AND CHAIN RING AND CUP STAR AND PEARL
Grocers and Teamen	BEEHIVE AND THREE SUGAR LOAVES (see Plate XXXVIII) BLACK BOY AND SUGAR LOAF CANISTER CANISTER AND THREE SUGAR LOAVES (see Plate XL) CHINA JAR (see Plate XC) COCOA TREE FAN AND CANISTER FIGG TREE AND SUGAR LOAF GOLDEN SUGAR LOAVES GREEN CANISTER ROSE AND THREE SUGAR LOAVES TEA CHEST TEA TUB, THREE SUGAR LOAVES AND CROWN (see Plate XXXIX) THREE SUGAR LOAVES
Gunmakers	CROSS BOW, ‖ CROSS GUNS
Hatters and Hosiers	BEAVER BISHOP BLAZE (see Plate XLVII) BLACK BOY AND HAT (see Plate XLIV) HAT AND CROSS DAGGERS KINGS ARMS AND BEAVER (see Plate XLV) STOCKING FRAME
Instrument Makers (Scientific)	GLOBE QUADRANT AND SPECTACLES ORRERY AND GLOBE SIR ISAAC NEWTON'S HEAD (see Plate XLVIII)

Trade	*Emblems employed*
Instrument Makers (Musical)	FRENCH HORN AND VIOLIN
	HAUTBOY AND TWO FLUTES
	TRUMPET AND HORNE (see page 8)
Nightmen and Polemen	GOLDEN POLE
Oilmen and Colourmen	OIL JAR
	OLIVE TREE AND COLOUR BARREL
	SHIP
Peruquiers	BLEW AND WHITE PERUKE
	HAND AND LOCKS OF HAIR
Perfumers	CIVET CAT
Scale Makers	ANGEL AND SCALE
	HAND AND SCALE (see Plate LXXXII)
Shoe Maker	ANGEL AND THREE SHOES (see Plate LXXXVI)
	PATTEN AND CROWN
	ROYAL BOOT
Stationers and Printsellers	GOLDEN PALLET
	THREE BIBLES AND DOVE (Arms of Stationers' Company)
Tallow and Wax Chandlers	BEEHIVE
	TALLOW CHANDLERS' ARMS (see Plate LXXXIX)
Tobacconists	TOBACCO ROLL
	TWO BLACK BOYS
Toymen	GREEN PARROT
Trunk Makers, Saddlers, etc.	CURRIERS' ARMS
	SADDLERS' ARMS
	SKINNERS' ARMS
	THREE RABBITS
	THREE TRUNKS AND BLUE BOAR
Turners	CROWN AND BOWL
	TURNERS' ARMS (see Plate XCV)
Writing Masters and Scriveners	HAND AND PEN

CHAPTER V

ARCHITECTURE AND COSTUME

ARCHITECTURE

The Architectural interest in Tradesmen's Cards is to be found mainly, as one might expect, in the engravings of the old shops and the street scenes in which these shops occur. A few, however, have as their salient feature some well-known edifice, others again present careful and quite architectural drawings of their new shop buildings, with the evident intention of drawing the notice of the public to their newest developments.

Of those using the landmark, or well-known building, as a means of fixing their locality in the minds of their customers, the earliest and perhaps the most interesting example is that shown on Plate LI, issued by William Conaway near the *Bull Head* in Dean Street By St. Ann's Church, Soho. He is a lamp-lighter by trade, and the engraving shows him mounted on a ladder tending the lamps in front of a nobleman's mansion, while his assistant replenishes the oil containers below. The interest, however, is focussed not on these entertaining little figures in their kneebreeches and three-cornered hats, but on the fine house which fills the panel, and this is used by the artist to give cachet to the lamp-lighter and define the quality of his clients. For this purpose the house is well chosen. It is Monmouth House, designed by Sir Christopher Wren, on the South Side of Soho Square, originally called 'King's Square,' and it was built in 1681 by the Duke of Monmouth, the natural son of Charles II, who was beheaded in 1685. Wheatley, in his *London Past and Present,* refers to this house, and mentions that there is an engraving of it in Smith's *Antiquities of London.* In J. T. Smith's *Nollekens and His Times* will be found a good account of the building as he saw it when the workmen were beginning to demolish it in 1773. 'In front was a spacious courtyard for carriages, and there were eight rooms on the ground floor.'

Exactly the same engraving appears on a Card in the Banks Collection in the British Museum, except that it bears the superscription of one Joel Iles, who, appropriately to his patronymic, was an Oilman in Queen Street, Soho Square. Otherwise the Cards are identical, even to the invidious reference to 'Persons of Quality and others.' Miss Banks has written under this Card, 'Monmouth House where

Bateman's Buildings now stand.' This is between Frith Street and Greek Street. Sir Joseph Banks resided at No. 32 Soho Square at the corner of Frith Street.

PLATE LXXXVII. Daniel Richards, Stationer, at St. Andrew's Church, Holborn, presents a clear elevation of the church on the south side of Holborn Viaduct. A church dedicated to St. Andrew has occupied this site since the twelfth century. Strype refers to it as having been rebuilt by Sir Christopher Wren in 1676. The tower was refaced with Portland stone in 1704, and the church was again restored in 1851 and 1872. The engraving on Daniel Richards' Card presents it as it was before the restorer had worked his will upon it.

Another landmark, though not a London one, is that of The Cross at Coventry. It was adopted by Mercers, doubtless on account of the close connection of the city of Coventry with their trade. A particularly fine engraving of it occurs on the large Card of 'William Atwick's Warehouse. *The Coventry Cross* in New Bond Street.' It is enclosed in a Chippendale frame, and it figures again, but in a more refined Adam type of frame, on that of his successors, Atwick & Son, at the same address, which is given as No. 149 New Bond Street in the London Directory of 1784. Another instance of this cross, though not nearly so good a drawing of it, is shown on the Card of 'Robert Taylor At *the Coventry Cross* near St. Margaret's Hill in the Borough, Southwark.' This again is a rather late Card, as it bears the street number of 94.

PLATE VI gives 'A Perspective View of David Loudon's Bunn House at Chelsey' drawn to scale. The design has been attributed to William Hogarth (see p. 68). This is a charming little building, long and low. It has only one floor to it. Running the whole length is a verandah supported by turned wooden columns with the Bun Shop set back under it. A delightful little restaurant which one would like to see in our parks to-day.

PLATE LII shows an interior, very fine and spacious, of Francis Noble's Circulating Library at *Otway's Head* in King Street, Covent Garden. The costume would date this at 1740-50. Another bookshop forty years or so later was a very celebrated one kept by Lackington Allen & Co. at the *Temple of the Muses* in Finsbury Square, which was built by the younger Dance in 1790. A Trade Card showing the exterior with its long range of fourteen tall round-headed windows claims it to be 'the finest shop in the world being 140 feet in front,' and another Card presents a very spacious room with a large circular counter standing in the centre of it under a dome round which runs a book-lined gallery. A staircase at the far end leads to the 'Lounging Rooms,' an amenity which we are apt to think is an innovation belonging to our modern Stores. In the foreground is the proprietor proudly displaying to a customer a scroll on which is written, 'A Section of the Dome,' evidently a notable feature of the new shop.

Other bookshops or, as they preferred to say, libraries, with all the charm of the late eighteenth-century small paned bow windows and delicate fanlights over the doors, are shown in the Cards of Tabart's Juvenile Library at 157 New Bond Street and The Eccentric Book Warehouse in St. John Street, presumably in Clerkenwell, for a coach is shown drawn up next door, and the inns in this thoroughfare were well-known rendezvous for stage-coaches and waggons.

A Printseller's shop, which stands to-day very much as it is shown in Archibald Robertson's Card, is at the entrance to Savile Row Passage. This was the house of Paul Sandby, the artist, and the Card is an aquatint by him. A note at the foot of the Card says, 'N.B. Sandbys works in Aqua Tinta to be had complete.' Beyond the shop is the entrance to Squibb's Auction Rooms, now occupied by the Alpine Club.

At the London Museum is to be seen an excellent example of one of these delicately bowed eighteenth-century shop fronts, and near to it hangs the Trade Card of 'S. Huntley, Linnen Draper at ye *Single Crown,*' who describes the place as 'A very Broad Fronted Shop Sashed in, almost over against ye East India House in Leadenhall Street.' One of the most charming of this type of card is that of John Flude, Pawnbroker and Silversmith, of Grace Church Street, which has a very delightful eighteenth-century shop front with well arranged exterior show-cases. It is illustrated in Plate LXXI. A prototype of the steel framed shop front with which we are familiar to-day is illustrated in the Trade Card of 'Gedge's Linen Draper's Shop at the corner of Cranbourne Alley and Leicester Square.' Originally known as the *Three Pigeons,* it became No. 1 Leicester Square. On the Card is written, 'This was the first front of a House set upon Iron Columns at the Year 1782.' It still retained the bowed windows with slight glazing bars, however.

In the nineteenth century illustrations of shop fronts became a much more common feature of the Tradesmen's Cards, and the transition from the old-fashioned shop fronts, which persisted into early Victorian times (as shown in Tallis's Street Views of 1838) down to the present day, can be traced.

The Eccentric BOOK WAREHOUSE S.^T JOHNS STREET.

Vaughn del.   Published June 1.st by Tegg & Co   Pugs Sc.^t

COSTUME

The representations of costumes which occur in Tradesmen's Cards often help us to assign a date when other indications are lacking. The Cards of Peruke-makers, Shoemakers, Hatters, and the like frequently show the fashions of the day, while the scenes depicted in the shops give a fairly accurate idea of the prevailing styles. It is therefore useful to have some rough idea of the sequence of the modes, and for this purpose an outline is given of the more outstanding changes in fashion covered by the illustrations.

CHARLES II

The Restoration in 1660 is marked by a great outburst of extravagance both in form and material. The doublet is slashed and curtailed to show the shirt of fine linen at waist and sleeve. Petticoat breeches, or wide breeches to the knee, are worn, and the whole is adorned with ruffles of lace and loops of ribbon. A broad brimmed hat covered with ribbons or feathers is fashionable. The great curled periwig comes in, and a small moustache with a point of beard on the chin is worn. The ladies, too, break away from Puritanism and discard the stiff wide collar for low dresses with elbow sleeves, slashed and tied with ribbons. The hair is elaborately dressed in ringlets standing out on each side of the face, with a row of little curls on the forehead. Patches are worn on the face.

In 1666 we get a great innovation, the advent of the frock-coat from the East, introduced, it is said, by John Evelyn to Charles II. It is a long straight coat from neck to knee with pockets very low down in front and is worn buttoned up.

JAMES II

In the next reign, James II (1685), the frock-coat becomes rather more shapely, and is the general wear. Faces are clean shaven from now on till the nineteenth century.

WILLIAM AND MARY

When William and Mary come in (1689) the coat gets fuller and stiffer in the skirts, which have now been slit up at the back for convenience in riding, and the coat is worn open, or partly open, to show the waistcoat, which is almost as long as the coat. The cuffs are deep and stiff. Periwigs have increased in size. By the middle of the reign the women's dress has changed considerably. The bodice is tight and long waisted, laced across the front over an undergown. The skirt is looped up at the sides to form panniers over the petticoat, and a 'pinner' or apron is often worn. The hair is dressed high over the forehead on a wire frame with one or two long curls falling on to the shoulders. An elaborately arranged cap, known as the 'fontange' or 'tower,' with stiff pleats rising vertically in tiers, completes the picture. Little muffs are carried by both men and women, and later there is a fashion for the women to wear coats of a masculine cut.

QUEEN ANNE

In the reign of Queen Anne (1702) the men's coats get tighter in the waists and the skirts become fuller at the sides. Hats are larger in the brim, which shows a tendency to turn up. Though the full wig is still worn, a simpler kind is also seen, and some are tied at the back; these begin to be powdered. With the ladies we get the hooped petticoat and a lower and simpler head-dress; aprons are still much worn and high red-heeled shoes. Trains tend to get shorter and hoops larger as time goes on.

GEORGE I

When George I came over from Hanover in 1714 the great periwig was already going out and its place being taken by the looped wig, white with powder. At this period the tied wig and one with a long tight queue are also in vogue. Coats are full in the skirt, the fullness being gathered in pleats at the side and hanging from a button just behind the pocket, which is now placed higher up. Both coat and waistcoat are worn open, buttoned only at the waist. Stockings are rolled over the knee, and shoe buckles are large. Women's hair is more simply done, gathered off the forehead with a knot of curls at the back, covered by a cap of lace or linen. This is occasionally tied at the chin or has lappets hanging at the back. Shallow crowned straw hats are worn over a cap. Hoops are large and bodices tight, but the new-fashioned sack-back dress, with wide pleats hanging from the shoulders, is coming into favour.

GEORGE II

By the time of George II (1727) the full-bottomed wig has quite disappeared, and various other shapes are being worn—the looped, the short curled, the long pigtailed wigs, and the curious bag wigs all find favour. Another vagary is for the tie to be brought round to the front of the neck and fastened with a solitaire. The long coat remains as in the previous reign, but there is also a short coat with stiffened skirts coming into use, which shows the tendency for the waist line and pockets to be higher than in earlier types.

The dressing of the ladies' hair remains small and close, and is worn with the milkmaid hat. The sack-back dress is at the height of its popularity in the Seventeen Fifties; it is set out at the sides, while the front and back are flat. Quilted petticoats are often worn, and flounces begin to come in at the end of this period.

GEORGE III

The accession of George III in 1760 ushers in a time of many changes. After a burst of extravagance (1773)—the Macaroni period—the wigs get simpler and gradually disappear. The full-skirted coat gives way to the tail coat without cuffs, and the waistcoat is quite short.

In the women's dress the period of extravagance is longer lived, the head-dresses become larger and even more elaborate than before. As these get higher and higher, hoops gradually disappear and their place is taken by the more elaborately made skirt with flounces and trimmings. The over-dress loses, bit by bit, the sack-back and becomes a tightly fitting bodice with the skirt still arranged over the petticoat in panniers. This fullness is gradually brought more and more towards the back until it becomes the bustle, and is balanced in front by the protruding fichu, completing the pouter pigeon profile.

FRENCH REVOLUTION

After the French Revolution in 1789 a great change comes over all dress, which now becomes very much simpler, and we get the tall slim lines of the Empire Period.

E. F. D. H.

For easy reference to the Plates the above information has been condensed into tabular form—see pages 34 and 35.

A Paper Stainer's Card showing Costume, *circa* 1750

Date.	Reign.	Plate.	Description of Costume.
1660	RESTORATION CHARLES II		Short slashed jacket petticoat, breeches, laces and ruffles, ribbons, great periwig, moustache and tiny beard.
			Women—low-necked dresses with slashed sleeves. Hair dressed in ringlets standing out each side of the face.
1666			The King sets the fashion for the frock-coat, long straight coat buttoned from neck to knee, pockets very low in front, baggy breeches.
1685	JAMES II	*See* p. ii	The new coat becomes slightly more shapely and is in general use. Faces are clean-shaven from now to 19th century.
1689	WILLIAM AND MARY		Coat stiffer and fuller in skirts, wide cuffs, not buttoned below waist. Full-bottomed wig, very large.
			Women—bodice tight and long waisted, laced over under dress, skirt looped up to form panniers, apron. Hair dressed high over frame, curls 'fontange.'
1702	ANNE		Coats fit closer in body, skirts fuller at sides. Smaller wigs and powder comes in.
		LIII	Women—hooped petticoats are worn with dress as before. Head-dress lower.

Date.	Reign.	Plate.	Description of Costume.
1714	GEORGE I	VI	Coat has fullness pleated at side, worn buttoned only at waist, also waistcoat. Powdered wigs of various shapes.
		XXXIV	Women—large hoops and tight bodices. Sack-back dress coming in. Hair more simply done and closer, covered with caps. Milkmaid hats.
		FRONT.	
1727	GEORGE II		Coat as in last reign and also a short coat with short stiff skirts. Tie and bag wigs and other shapes.
1740		LII	Women — sack-back dress over hoops at sides, front and back flat. Hair still close. Milkmaid hat with cap underneath still favoured.
		LXXVIII	
		XVII	
1745 1750		LXXIII	Sack-back dress reaches its height.
		See p. 33	Flounced skirts come in towards the end of this reign.
1760	GEORGE III	LXIX	In this reign the skirted coat gradually changes to the tail.
			Women—hoops die out and bustle comes in.
1773			Macaroni period. Head-dresses of both sexes high and fantastic.
1792	FRENCH REVOLUTION	See p. 29	Which marks a change towards simplicity in all dress.

CHAPTER VI

CURIOSITIES IN TRADESMEN'S CARDS

I HAVE said in the Preface that there are no books on Tradesmen's Cards, nor has the subject, so far as I know, been treated at any length in the Archæological Journals: even the indexes of *Notes and Queries* from 1850 to 1915 fail to provide any but the slightest of references. During the last fifteen years there have appeared in *Country Life* from time to time a few short articles on particular trades, and *The Connoisseur* has lately published two articles on Lord Winterton's Collection, by Mr. Richard Holworthy.

Apart from these scattered references the only account of these Cards would appear to be in the three volumes of *Rariora*, by that great collector, Mr. J. Eliot Hodgkin, and in those three volumes four pages only are devoted to Tradesmen's Cards. These are illustrated by seven plates. In these few pages, however, he has things to say which are of interest to the collector.

He calls them Early Shop Bills or Tradesmen's Cards. He tells us that in the Banks Collection at the British Museum there are 4388 specimens, and that his own collection comprised 2800, classed under 331 trades. He gives a list of those which he considers the more unusual trades, as follows:

Air Mill Makers	Fishermen
Arms Painters	Harmonisers of Musical
Astrologers	Instruments
Ballad Mongers	Ingrossers
Ban(d) Box Makers	Lunatic Keepers
Calculators (of chances in	Nightmen
lotteries)	Oculists
Chimney Sweeps	Pedometer Makers
Chiropedal Car Makers	Prize Fighters
Coach Trumpet Makers	Quacks
Court Plaster Makers	Sergeants at Mace
Cuppers	Slop Makers
Dog Doctors	Ventriloquists
Fencing Masters	Worm Makers

He then gives a list of 'the more important or more prolific among engravers of Tradesmen's Cards,' which is as follows:

Aveline, Bartolozzi, Bickham, Canot, Cardon, Choffard, Clee, Cole, Cross, Darly, Darling, Deuchar, Fitler, Fourdrinier, Gribelin, Hancock, Hogarth, Kirk, Kirkall, Longmate, Morrison, Pye, Schiavonetti, Sherborn, Sherwin, Skinner, Stent, Vivares, and Yates.

He refers to his ancillary collections of Tobacco Papers and Watch Papers, and he says that it has been his intention to write a Monograph on Tradesmen's Cards, and has collected material for it, but that it must be 'probably altogether abandoned,' which is much to be regretted, for he had amassed what is probably the largest collection on this subject which has been put together since the days of Sir Joseph Banks. In the course of his short article he makes the following statements, which must carry weight:

'Very few people know anything at all about the earlier descriptions of Shop Bills or have even seen an example. . . . Let no man deride such a collection as consisting of trivial or unprofitable material. Whatever be the extent of his previous knowledge of the work of engravers of ornament of the period which it covers, that knowledge will be enormously increased by a study of the diversity of their work in a field so largely their own, and he will be able to trace in a much fuller degree than in the case of Ex Libris the change of style almost from decade to decade, its gradual degradation and ultimate debasement. He will in the second place acquire a knowledge, more easily gained in this way than in any other, of the changes in fashion in, and of the strange names of, many of the articles offered by the various dealers; and will derive much amusement as well as much information from the quaint devices and wording by which the capabilities of the traders are glorified.'

Whether or no we can go quite all the way with Mr. Hodgkin in finding glorification for the capabilities of the trader in the 'quaint devices' he employed for his wares, it is at all events interesting to record the names of some of his wares which have now become obsolete and to note trades mentioned in the Cards which have fallen into disuse. I have therefore put together from time to time a miscellaneous collection of such items—odd trades, unusual Signs, obsolete wares, curious details and turns of phrase occurring on various Cards which are likely to be of interest to the collector.

To those who have not yet known the fascination of Trade Card collecting, these memoranda will give some indication of the wide range of interest covered in this pursuit. That such a list should include 'shoes and ships and sealing wax' is to be expected, but one may not have realized that there were such pleasant trades as that of the Spatterdash Maker, or may have forgotten, perhaps, that there existed Rocking-horse Makers, or again, one may have been happily ignorant that there was so grim a one as that of Skeleton Seller. Unless one had actually seen the Card of Thomas Collyer, one could hardly believe that there was so delightfully fantastic a calling as that of a 'Haberdasher of Hatts.'

On the following pages, therefore, will be found a miscellany of notes that I have made from time to time in looking through various collections. I have put down any trades which struck me as being out-of-the-way or which are no longer practised, old-fashioned wares no longer in demand, with the quaint names by which they were known, Signs which are in some way curious, and any turns of phrase peculiar to the times and now fallen into disuse. They are the merest jottings.

MEMORANDA
OF CURIOUS OR OBSOLETE TRADES AND WARES, TOGETHER WITH NOTES OF UNUSUAL SIGNS AND QUAINT EXPRESSIONS MET WITH ON TRADESMEN'S CARDS

Academies

'YOUNG GENTLEMEN ARE INSTRUCTED IN THE VARIOUS BRANCHES OF ENGLISH AND FRENCH, INCLUDING WASHING, BOOK KEEP-ING, ALGEBRA AND MATHEMATICS, AND THE USE OF THE GLOBES. THIRTY POUNDS PER ANNUM.

N.B.—YOUNG GENTLEMEN WEARING LIGHT TROUSERS ETC. THE WASHING WILL BE 10/- PER YEAR EXTRA.

TO INSTRUCT THE YOUTHFUL MIND IN MORAL AND RELIGIOUS PRINCIPLES FORMS AN ESSENTIAL PART OF THE RULES OF THIS SEMINARY.'

Academies (*contd.*)   'TEACHER OF THE MATHEMATICS AND MNE-
MONICS.'

Accoutrement Maker
and Sword Cutler

Agent in Naval Affairs   MOTTO 'LET US BANG THE DONS.'
'TRANSACTS OFFICERS', SEAMEN AND MARINERS'
BUSINESS OR FOR THEIR RELATIONS.'

Anchor Smith

Apothecary and Surgeon

Aquarellist   PAUL SANDBY, ST. GEORGE'S ROW, OXFORD
TURNPIKE. (Aquatint with view of Turn-
pike.)

Artist   PAINTER OF MINIATURES.

Archill-maker   (Archil—A dye made from lichens.)   Dated
1742.

Artificial Eye Maker   See p 21.

Asses' Milk   PURVEYOR OF. THOS EDWARDS, AT THE *Ass
and Foal,* THE BOTTOM OF WIGMORE STREET,
MARYLEBONE LANE, NEAR CAVENDISH
SQUARE. (Dated 1781.) (See Plate XXV.)

'BOUGHT OR SOLD OR LET BY THE MONTH. OR
ASSES DROVE TO ANY PERSONS HOUSE IN
TOWN OR COUNTRY. BY JAMES JONES AT THE
Ass and Foal FACING *Bird in Hand* IN WOOD'S
CLOSE.'

Attorney-at-law

Back Maker (? Cooper)   'SELLS BELL AND BOUGE VATTS, WORM
TUBS, ETC.'

Backgammon Table
Maker

Bathing Machines   'AMIDAS AND MARY SURFLEN AT MARGATE IN
KENT. M. SURFLEN ATTENDS THE LADIES
HERSELF AS GUIDE.'

Baths

THE KING'S (James II) BAGNIO, LONG ACRE. (Dated 1686.)

'TO ALL GENTLEMEN LOVERS OF SWIMMING AND BATHING. THIS IS TO GIVE NOTICE. THAT THERE IS DISCOVERED BEHIND THE BOWLING GREEN IN OLD STREET NEAR ST. LUKE'S CHURCH THE BATHING WATERS OF THE PEERLESS POOL' . . . . (Dated 1743.)

Bed Joyner

Bellows Maker

Bombazine Maker

Booksellers

WILLIAM SANDBY AT *The Ship* WITHOUT TEMPLE BAR. *The Ship* next Falcon Court was occupied in 1756 by Wm. Sandby, who afterwards became a partner in the banking house of Snow and Denne in the Strand. He sold the good-will in 1768 to John McMurray, who there founded the famous publishing business of John Murray & Co. It afterwards migrated to Albemarle Street in 1812. (See Timperley's *Printers' Manual*.)

A Card of John Murray, 'SUCCESSOR TO MR. SANDBY, BOOKSELLER AND STATIONER AT NO. 32 OVER AGAINST ST. DUNSTAN'S CHURCH IN FLEET STREET.'

(See Curwen's *Booksellers Old and New*.)

An early Trade Card of Ward & Chandler, Booksellers, at the same address, was issued about 1734.

HARVEY, 4 ST. JAMES STREET. Card designed by George Cruikshank, 1872.

Boot and Shoe Maker

'DOUBLE AND SINGLE CHANNEL PUMPS, SPATTERDASHES, CLOGS AND PATTENS.'

Bow and Arrow Maker

'C. TOMEZ, BOW AND ARROW MAKER, TEACHER OF ARCHERY, THROWING THE JAVELIN, ETC. NO. 15 SUSSEX STREET, BEDFORD SQUARE.'

Brass Cannon Maker	
Braziers	'THOMAS PICKETT, CITIZEN AND BRAZIER AT THE *Sign of ye Frying Pan.*' (See Plate III.) 'AT THE SIGN OF *The Three Cocks.* ALL SORTS AND SIZES OF COCKS MADE NEAT AND CHEAP.'
Breeches Maker	'WILLM. TURTLE BREECHES MAKER AND GLOVER. N.B.—NO BUSINESS DONE ON THE SABBATH SUCH AS BUYING AND SELLING.'
Bricklayer	
Brick-Mould Maker in General	'*At the Bear and Ragged Staff,* WHITECROSS STREET, ALSO MAKES PAVING BRICK, MOULDS BATH STOVES, ETC.'
Bright Smith	'AT YE SIGN OF *ye Smoak Jack.*'
Buckle Maker	'THE NEW INVENTED BLACK BARR BUCKLES.'
Bugg Destroyer	'ELEANOR BRAINIFF—DAUGHTER AND SUCCESSOR TO HER LATE FATHER GEORGE BRIDGES, BUGG DESTROYER TO HIS MAJESTY.'
Bun Bakers	(See Plates V and VI.)
Cabinet Makers	'PETER LANGLOIS IN TOTTENHAM COURT ROAD, NEAR WINDMILL STREET, MAKES ALL SORTS OF FINE CABINETS AND COMMODES MADE AND INLAID IN THE POLITEST MANNER WITH BRASS AND TORTOISESHELL.' Below appears a translation into French, but omitting 'in the politest manner.' 'BED CORNISHES,' 'TEASTERS,' 'BEAUROES AND FIELD BEDS,' 'FASHIONABLE STANDING BEDS,' 'CHAMBER TABLES,' 'TEA BOARDS.' 'CHANDELIERS AND LANTHORNS IN BRASS AT THE LOWEST PRICES.' THOS. SHERATON. (See Drawing Master.) 'FUHRLONG, CABINET MAKER IN THE MODERN GRECIAN AND CHINESE TASTE, 5 TOTTENHAM COURT ROAD.'
Calendrer	'ORRIS CLEANER AND SCOWERER.'

Calico Printer	See Plate IX.
Candlestick Maker	'WAX TAPER STANDS, LUSTRES AND CANDELA-BRA.'
Case Maker	'ALL SORTS OF SHAGREEN, NURSES, FISHSKIN AND MAHOGANY KNIFE CASES, SMELLING AND DRAM BOTTLES, CANISTER CASES IN BLUE OR GREEN DOGSKIN MOUNTED IN SILVER.'
Chemists	'CHYMICAL AND GALENICAL MEDICINES, WITH ALL SORTS OF DRUGGS. N.B. THE ELIXIR FOR THE ASTHMA AS ALSO FOR THE GOUT AND RHUMATISM.' (See Plate XI.)
	'WILLIAM BLACKWELL AT *Ye Buckthorn Tree*, COVENT GARDEN. SELLS ALL SORTS OF PHYSICAL HERBS, ROOTS, FLOWERS AND SEEDS, GREEN AND DYED BUCKTHORN, ELDERBURYS AND JUICE, LEECHES AND VIPERS. WHOLESALE AND RETAIL.'
	'*At the Sign of the Elaboratory.*'
Chimney Sweeps	'JEANE TEMPELL, CHIMBLEY-SWEEPERS AT THE SIGNE OF *The Woman Chimbley Sweper*, IN NUTNERS STREET, NEAR THE WATCH HOUSE IN HOLBORN.' (See p. viii.)
	'CURES SMOAKING CHIMNEY'S IN TOWN OR COUNTRY. NO CURE NO PAY.' (See Plate XII.)
	' . . . TO SEVERAL OF HIS MAJESTY'S OFFICES, AND NIGHTMAN TO HIS R.H. THE PRINCE OF WALES.'
China Rivetter	'EDMUND MORRIS AT *The China Jar* IN GRAY'S INN PASSAGE COMING INTO RED LION SQUARE, HOLBOURNE. MAKES ALL SORTS OF CHINA WARES WITH A PECULIAR ART WHICH HAS NEVER BEFORE BEEN FOUND OUT IN THIS KINGDOM SO AS A RIVETTED PIECE OF CHINA WILL DO AS MUCH SERVICE AS WHEN NEW. AS THERE ARE MANY IMPOSTERS BOTH IN TOWN AND COUNTRY THAT MAKE FALSE

China Rivetter (*contd.*)   PRETENSIONS, I DESIRE NO OTHER SATISFAC-
TION THAN WHAT WORKMANSHIP MERITS.

N.B.—IF ANY OF MY WORK SHOULD COME TO
PIECES WITHIN 20 OR 30 YEARS I WILL
REPAIR IT WITHOUT ANY FURTHER EXPENSE.'

Chocolate Maker   'THE ONLY MAKERS OF SIR HANS SLOANE'S MILK
CHOCOLATE. EDWARD AND JOHN WHITE,
8 GREEK STREET, SOHO.'

Clock Maker   'PINCHBECK, SENR. CLOCK, WATCH MAKER
AND TOYMAN AT *Pinchbeck's Head* IN FLEET
STREET. ONLY MAKER OF THE TRUE AND
GENUINE METAL.'

Clog Maker   'LEATHER CLOGGS, FINE LEATHER PATTENS,
CORKE CLOGGS FOR LADIES.' (See Plate XV.)

Coach Spring Maker

Coach Trumpet Maker

Coach Wheeler

Coalman   'AT *the Old Collier and Cart* AT FLEET DITCH
NEAR HOLBORN.' (See Plate XVIII.)

Coffee Houses

Coffin Plate Chaser

Confectioners   'AT *the Pine Apple* IN BERKELEY SQUARE,
CEDRATI AND BERGAMOT CHIPS, NAPLES
DIAVOLINI AND DIAVOLONI. COMMON SUGAR
PLUMS, SYRUP OF CAPILAIRE, ORGEATE AND
MARSH MALLOW, GHIMAVE OR LOZENGES FOR
COLDS.' (See Plate XX.)

'APRICOCKS,' 'JORDON ALMONDS,' 'RAYSONS,'
'DROGEA,' 'COMFITS AND FLOWER CANDY.'

'HARTS HORN JELLIES AND BLOMANGES,'
'SHERBERTS,' 'ROUT CAKES,' 'ICE CREAM
WHIPS AND BLANSHMANGE.'

Cork Maker   CORK CUTTERS.

Corn Cutter and Nail
   Operator

Cooper in General	'BATHING TUBS LENT AND SOLD.'
Costumier	AT *ye Harlequin and Pierrot.*
Covent Garden Porter	
Cowkeeper and Dairyman	'IN COVENTRY COURT IN THE HAYMARKET.'
Cricket Ball and Patten Maker	
Cupper	'WHERE GENTLEMEN MAY BE ACCOMODATED (IF NOT FULL) WITH LODGING, SWEATING AND BATHING OR CUPPING. AND WITH THE UTMOST DECORUM. THERE IS LIKEWISE A GOOD COLD BATH.' (See Plate XXIII.)
Currier and Leather-Seller	'WILLIAM KIPPIAX, FELLMONGER AND LEATHER DRESSER. BUCK LEATHER BREECHES, RAMS AND CALVES DREST IN OIL OR ALLUM.' (Displays the Arms of the Skinners' Company.)
Cutlers	AT *the Red M. and Dagger* IN POPE'S HEAD ALLEY. (See p. 16, and also compare Plate LXXXI.) See under Razor Makers.
	'EQUIPAGES,' 'CANE HEADS,' 'STANDISHES,' 'PROSPECTIVE GLASSES.'
	'ALEXANDER JOLLY AT *The Unicorn and Case of Knives* IN COMPTON STREET, SOHO. TINDER BOXES, TOOTHPICK CASES, GUN HAMMERS, SQUIRREL-CHAINS, POUN BOXES, HUNTING HORNS, POWDER HORNS AND DRINKING HORNS, SHOT POUCHES, GUN FLINTS AND THE BEST BATTLE GUNPOWDER.'
	'QUADRILL BOXES,' 'POWDER ENGINES,' 'BACK-GAMMON TABLES,' 'WIG SPRINGS,' AND 'INK HORNS.'
	'SAW STROPS,' 'FLEAMS,' 'SNUFF BOXES,' 'STEEL AND BATH METAL SHOE BUCKLES,' 'CHALK LINES AND LINE ROWLS.' 'JEWS HARPS,' 'HOG AND PIG RINGS,' 'HORN BOOK PRIM-MERS,' 'TOBACCO TONGS,' 'FOUNTAIN PENS,'

Cutlers (*contd.*)	'DRAM BOTTLES,' 'PERSPECTIVE GLASSES,' 'SLATE-BOOKS,' 'VELLUM BOOKS,' 'BRASS JAGGERS,' 'HAWK BELLS,' 'CHAMBER BELLS,' 'RING AND POST DIALS.'

At the Sign of the Tare. (Dated 1698.)

Dancing Master	'DANCING BOTH SERIOUS AND COMICK TAUGHT BY MR. LOFT, LIKEWISE HORNPIPES, FENCING AND MUSIC.'
Dentist	'SURGEON DENTIST TO HIS MAJESTY. FAMILIES ATTENDED BY THE YEAR. SAMUEL DARKIN YE ELDER OPERATOR OF TEETH AND SAMUEL DARKIN THE YOUNGER BLEEDER AND OPERATOR OF TEETH; ALSO CUPS AT THE SIGN OF THE BLEEDER AND STAR.'
Drapers	'ALLOPEENS,' 'ALLAMODES,' 'ARMOZEENS,' AND 'FIGURED AMENS.'
	'BOMBAZINES,' 'BURDETS,' 'BROGLIOS,' 'BARRAGONS.'
	'CALLIMANCOES,' 'CAMBLETS,' 'CHERRY-DERRYS.'
	'DUFFELL JOSEPHS,' 'DUFFEL FOR CLOAKS AND CARDINALS,' 'CLOUTINGS,' 'DUCAPES,' 'DONYARS,' 'DURANTS,' 'DUFFINS,' 'DIMATHEES,' 'DORSETEENS,' 'DOWLACE.'
	'EVERLASTINGS.'
	'FLORETTAS,' 'FLORIDOS.'
	'GARLICKS,' 'STRIPED GHENTINGS,' 'GARTERINGS,' 'GAUZES FOR CAPUCHINES,' 'GROGRAMS.'
	'HOOP COATS,' 'HUGABACKS,' 'HOOPING HOLLANDS.'
	'INKLE.'
	'JEANS.'
	'LUTESTRINGS STRIP'D AND SPRIG'D,' 'LONG LAWNS.'
	'MINIONETTE LAWNS.'

Drapers (*contd.*)

'MESSINETS,' 'MISSENTS,' 'MECKLENBERGS,' 'MANTUAS.'

'NONE-SO-PRETTIES.'

'OSNABURGS.'

'PRUNELLAS,' 'PEELINGS,' 'PADUSOYS,' 'POLLI-CATS,' 'PERRIWIG-RIBBON.'

'QUILTED PETTICOATS,' 'WHALEBONED PETTI-COATS,' 'QUILTED AND HOOP PETTYCOATS,' 'FINE SCARLET CLOTH VELVET HOODS,' 'TURKISH AND SULTAN GOWNS MADE AFTER THE BEST MANNER.' 'MEN'S GOWNS AND BANYANS.'

'ROCCELOES,' 'RASDEMORIS,' 'RATTEENS,' 'ROS-SLES.'

'SHALLOONS,' 'SHAGREENS,' 'STOMACHERS,' 'SILVERETS,' 'SHAGGS,' 'SAGATHYS,' 'SERGE-DUSOYS.'

'TIFFANYS,' 'FLOWERED AND PLAIN TABBIES,' 'TABBYNETS.'

'REAL NINE TIMES DYED BLUE FLANNEL FOR THE GOUT AND RHEUMATISM.'

WOOLLEN DRAPER *at the Hand and Sheers* IN THE BOROUGH.

'*At the Two Fustian Rolls, Rose and Crown,*' WHITE HORSE YARD, DRURY LANE.

'*Pack Horse and Fustian Roll.*'

'*At the D'Oyley's Head.*' (With Portrait of D'Oyley.)

Drawing Master

T. SHERATON, 106 WARDOUR STREET, SOHO, 1795.

'TEACHES PERSPECTIVE, ARCHITECTURE AND ORNAMENTS. MAKES DESIGNS FOR CABINET MAKERS AND SELLS ALL KINDS OF DRAWING BOOKS.'

The celebrated Furniture Designer. He died No. 8 Broad Street, Golden Square, 1806; also lived at 41 Davies Street (Grosvenor Square) in 1793, and at 98 Wardour Street.

Druggist	'FRESH SPAW AND PYRMONT WATERS.'
Edge Tool Maker	
Elephants' Teeth	Dealers in.
Engineers	Illustrations of Hand Pumps and Printing Presses, Agricultural Implements, Patent Pendulum Steam Engine, Beam Engine, Hand Looms, Early Power Looms, Paddle Steamers.
Engravers	'WM. AND CLUER DICEY *at the Maidenhead* IN BOW CHURCH YARD. SHOPKEEPERS BILLS ARE CURIOUSLY ENGRAV'D.' (See Plate XXIX.) 'W. HOGARTH AT *ye Golden Ball* YE CORNER OF CRANBOURNE ALLEY, LITTLE NEWPORT STREET.' (Dated 1720.)
Engravers' Punch Maker	
Fan Maker	AT THE *Fan and Dove.*
Feather Bed Maker	
Fell monger and Leather Dresser	
Firework Makers	'BENJAMIN CLITHEROE, FIRE WORKER, REAL ENGINEER TO CUPERS AND MARY LE BONE GARDENS. MAKES AND FURNISHES NOBLE-MEN, GENTLEMEN, ETC., WITH ALL SORTS OF ARTIFICIAL FIREWORKS AFTER YE ITALIAN AND CHINA METHOD IN YE NEATEST TASTE AT THE LOWEST PRICES. HAS THE REAL TRUE AND GENUINE CHINA FIRE y^t REPRESENTS A BEAUTIFUL FRUIT TREE IN FULL BLOOM, WILL THROW ITS FLOWERS FROM 10 TO 30 FEET HIGH. THE SMALL ONES MAY BE FIRED IN ROOMS WITHOUT DANGER.' 'MORTRAM. DECORATIVE PAINTER AND ARTIST IN FIREWORKS. COATS OF ARMS, MAGNIFI-CENT TEMPLES, TRIUMPHAL ARCHES, SEA FIGHTS, ETC. EXECUTED IN FIRE WORKS SO

Firework Makers (*contd.*)	AS TO PRODUCE THE MOST BEAUTIFUL EFFECT.'
Fire Engine Maker	JOHN BRISTOW, RATCLIFFE HIGHWAY. (See Plate XXXI.)
	'A PROSPECTIVE VIEW OF PART OF THE RUINS OF THE LATE DREADFUL FIRE WHICH HAPPENED IN CORNHILL, MARCH 25. 1748.'
Fishing Tackle Makers	'WILLIAM BROWNE *At the Sign of the Fish.*' (See p. ii.)
	'MARY KNIGHT AND SON *At the Old Compleat Angler*—A CORNER SHOP IN CROOKED LANE.'
	'JOHN CHESHIRE AND WILL BUSICK *at the Angler and Trout* IN CROOKED LANE, MAKERS OF FISHING TACKLE, HOOKS, LIKEWISE BEST WHITE CHAPPEL NEEDLES FOR TAYLORS, STAYMAKERS, GLOVERS, MILLINERS, SURGEONS AND NEEDLES FOR DYERS, HOTT PRESSERS, SAIL MAKERS, SOW GELDERS. ANY COUNTRY CHAPMEN MAY BE AS WELL USED BY SENDING A LETTER AS IF PRESENT THEMSELVES.'
	ONESIMUS USTONSON, BELL YARD, FLEET STREET.
Flax Dresser	
Floor Cloth Painter	
Frame Maker	'AT *the Architrave Frame.*'
Frock Shop	'MARY AND ANN HOGARTH. SELL YE BEST AND MOST FASHIONABLE READY MADE FROCKS, SUITS OF FUSTIAN TICKEN OR HOLLAND, STRIPP'D DIMITY AND FLANNEL WAISTCOATS, BLUE AND CANVAS FROCKS AND BLUECOAT BOYS DRA^{rs}.' (See Plate XXXIV.)
Furriers	'MUFFS, TIPPETS, FURR CAPS, BEAR SKINS FOR COACH SEATS.'
	'CAPARISON FURNITURE FOR SADDLERS.'
Girdler	'AT y^e *Whale & Raven* NEXT DOOR TO BOW CHURCH.'

Goldsmiths	'ELLIS GAMBLE *at the Golden Angel* IN CRAN-BOURN STREET, LEICESTER FIELDS.' (See Plate XXXV.)

'At *the Golden Angel* in Leicester Fields lived Ellis Gamble the Goldsmith, to whom Hogarth was apprenticed to learn the art of silver plate engraving. A Shop Bill engraved by Hogarth is greatly coveted by collectors.' (See Wheatley's *London Past and Present*.)

Ireland the engraver is said to have considered his own impression of this Card to be unique—it is certainly extremely rare.

PETER DE LA FONTAINE *at the Golden Cup* IN LITCHFIELD STREET, SOHO. Card engraved by Hogarth. (See Frontispiece.)

'WILLM. HARDY IN RATCLIFFE HIGHWAY NEAR SUN TAVERN FIELDS.' (Engraved by Hogarth.)

'WM. AND MARY DEARDS AT *The Star*, THE END OF PALL MALL NEAR ST. JAMES' HAYMARKET.

À *l'Etoile* AU BOUT DE PELLEMÊLE PRÈS DU MARCHÉ AU FOIN DE ST. JACQUES.'

Gold Beater	*At the Golden Hammer.*
Grocers and Tea Men	FINE HYSON, PEKOE, SOUCHONG, COUGON, BOHEA, BLOOM AND COMMON TEAS. FINEST BRISTOL AND DOUBLE LOAVES, CLAY'D AND ALL OTHER SUGARS. SALOOP.

'PORTABLE SOUP'—an early form of tinned food.

Gunsmiths	'JEFFERY DUNN, GUN MAKER AT *ye Cross Bow* IN YE HAYMARKET.' (See title page.)

'FOR SALE AT *The White Bear* WAREHOUSE, PICCADILLY. A LARGE ASSORTMENT OF FIRE ARMS AMONG WHICH ARE SEVERAL EXCELLENT FOWLING PIECES WITH TWISTED BARRELS, GOLD TOUCH HOLES, ETC. ALSO

Gunsmiths (*contd.*)	GREAT VARIETY OF NEW INVENTED SPRING GUNS FOR WAREHOUSES, GARDENS, PLANTATIONS, ETC. CROSS BOWS, MUSKETS, SHOTS AND FLINTS, PERCUSSION LOCKS, COPPER CAPS AND PRIMERS. BARRELS NEWLY BORED AND BREECH'D. PATENT LOCKS AND REAL DAMASCUS BARR^{LS}.'
Haberdashers	'BREEDS AND BUSKS,' 'CAULS FOR PERIWIGS,' 'PURL AND COXCOMB CAWLS,' 'PERUKE RIBBONS,' 'CYPRESS AND CAT GUT,' 'FRENCH PATCHES,' 'ROLES,' 'WIERS,' 'FERRITS,' 'FANCIED TIPPETS,' 'WRAPPERS,' 'CARDINALS' AND 'POLINEES,' 'PERSIAN BODKINS,' 'JETT STOMACHERS,' 'SLEEVE KNOTS,' 'LACINGS,' 'GARTERINGS,' 'FLOWERED SILK FOR CAPUCHINS,' 'HAIR BINDS AND SILK KNEE BANDS.'
Hackney Men	
Harness Maker and Enterer	
Harp String Maker	
Hatters	THOMAS COLLYER 'HABERDASHER OF HATTS. HATTER AND SWORD CUTLER. BEAVER HAT MANUFACTORY. REAL HAT MAKER.' (See Plate XLV.)

' JOHN WEST HAT MAKER AT *the Beaver and Star,* THE CORNER OF MONMOUTH STREET, NEXT THE BROADWAY, ST. GILES', FURNISHES GENTLEMEN WITH THE LOAN OF 3 GOOD NEW HATS IN THE YEAR KEPT IN PROPER REPAIR FOR 15^s AND UPWARDS TO £1. 1^s EACH WARRANTED WORTH WITHIN 3^s OF THE SUM AGREED FOR. HATS DYED, DREST AND COCKED IN THE GENTEELEST MANNER.'

'WILLOW HATS.' 'BEST BEAVER FOR 18^s.'

'AT NOYES'S HAT AND STAY WAREHOUSE, *The Hat, Bonnet and Stay* IN FORE STREET.'

Hatters (*contd.*)

'GILES HAT WAREHOUSE AT THE *Golden Lace Hat* 3 GLASSHOUSE STREET.'

Subsequently became Gill & Johnson's, now Herbert Johnson's, 38 New Bond St.

LEGHORN STRAW HATS. J. SPERATIS, 54 PALL MALL. (Engraved by F. Bartolozzi.)

Herald and House Painter

Honey Warehouse

'RICH^d. HOY AT HIS HONEY WAREHOUSE 175 PICCADILLY SELLS BOX AND GLASS BEEHIVES CONTRIVED SO AS LADIES MAY HAVE THEM ON THEIR DRESSING TABLES WITHOUT THE LEAST DANGER OF BEING STUNG.'

Hoop Maker

'TO HER MAJESTY.'

Hosiers

'THOMAS MOORE MARCHAND FABRICANT DE BAS ET BONNETERIE *à l'Enseigne de l' Evesque Blaze* DANS CHISWELL STREET. . . . GANS ET MITAINES DE COTON FIL, SOŸE ET LAINE.' (See Plate XLVII.)

'MITS AND MUFFATEES,' 'BLUE AND STRIP'D LINSEES,' 'BAYS,' 'SWANSKIN,' ETC.

'HOSIER, HAT MAKER ALSO VENDOR OF LOTTERY TICKETS.'

'GEORGE PAYNE HOSIER AND MANUFACTURER 80 NEWGATE ST.'

His Card reproduces the old carved stone panel of Charles II's Porter and Dwarf, dated 1669.

'This Sign used to stand over the entrance to Bull Head Court, Newgate Street . . . the figures were painted, their coats being red, the King's Livery, and their waistcoats blue.' (See Norman's *London Signs and Inscriptions*.)

Notes and Queries, 25 July, 1903, mentions this house as being No. 78 Newgate St.

Hosiers (*contd.*)

NEWHAM AND THRESHER HOSIERS AT *The Peacock*. NO. 152 NEXT DOOR TO SOMERSET HOUSE, STRAND.

(This old family business is still carried on at No. 152, under the style of Thresher and Glenny.)

Indigo Dealer

Inns, etc.

'NEAT POST CHAISES,' 'STAGE COACHES,' 'RIGHT USQUEBAUGH GREEN AND YELLOW,' 'FINE ORANGE SHRUBB,' 'CITRON WATER,' 'BATAVIA ARRACK,' 'RATAFIA AND SEVERAL OTHER FINE CORDIALS.'

Instrument Makers

'PHILOSOPHICAL, MATHEMATICAL AND OPTICAL.' (See Plate XLVIII.)

'ORRERYS,' 'QUADRANTS,' 'AZIMUTH COMPASSES,' 'SLIDING GUNTER'S SCALES.'

Ironmongers

'THOMAS PICKETT, CITIZEN AND BRAZIER.' (See Plate III.)

'ROBERT HARDING IRONMONGER BRAISER AND SWORN APPRAISER AT THE *Stow Grate* NEAR TO THE BREW-HOUSE IN THE GREAT MINORIES.'

'CHOCOLATE AND DRINKING POTS,' 'PUMKIN OR WARMING PANS,' 'POTTAGE POTS,' 'TINDER BOXES,' 'FLAT CANDLESTICKS OF THE NEWEST FASHION,' 'EXTINGUISHERS,' 'BOX DIALS,' 'PENCIL CASES AND YE NEWEST FOUNTAIN PENS,' 'CHAMBER GRATES,' 'STOW GRATES,' 'SMOAK JACKS,' 'MAN TRAPS.'

Italian Warehousemen

'LEGORNE HATS,' 'LUTE AND VIOLIN STRINGS,' 'BOOKS OF ESSENCES,' 'VENICE TREACLE,' 'BALSOMES,' 'FLORENCE CORDIALS,' 'BOLOGNIA SAUSIDGES AND NAPLE SOAP.'

Itinerant Printseller

Japanners

'JOHN JUKES DOES ALL MANNER OF JAPAN WORK, MENDS OLD JAPAN AND MAKES IT FRESH AS NEW. SECURES INDIA JAPAN IN YE NEATEST MANNER.'

Lacemen	'MAKES ALL SORTS OF SHOULDER KNOTS IN GOLD SILVER SILK OR WORSTED OFFICERS AND SERJEANTS SWASHES. FIFE STRINGS IN THE NEATEST TASTE.'
Lamplighter	(See Plate L.)
Landscape and Portrait Painter	
Lantern Maker	'FURNISHETH PERSONS OF QUALITY AND OTHERS WITH LAMPS, LANTHORNS AND IRONS. ALSO KEEPS SERVANTS TO LIGHT THEM AT REASONABLE RATES.' (See Plate LI.)
Lapidary	
Leather Pipe and Bucket Maker	Dated 1782.
Lighterman and Coal Dealer	
Man-Midwife	
Mantua Maker	
Menagerie	
Mercers	(See Drapers.)
'Messenger of Bankruptcy'	
Mill Maker	'*At the Dial, Mill and Hand-screw* IN TOOLEY ST., NEAR YE BRIDGE-FOOT, SOUTHWARK. 'MALT MILLS, SNUFF MILLS, COCHENEAL AND INDIGO MILLS, BARK MILLS, ALMOND MILLS, ETC.'
Music Master	'TEACHER OF THE HARP AND BARD TO THE PRINCE REGENT AT THE OFFICE OF ROBES IN THE LORD STEWARD'S COURTYARD IN ST. JAMES' PALACE.'
Musical Instrument Makers	'ALL SORTS OF TRUMPETTS AND KETTLE DRUMS, FFRENCH HORNS, SPEAKING TRUMPETTS, HEARING HORNES FOR DEAFE PEOPLE AND ALL SORTS OF POWDER FLASKS AND ALLSO

Musical Instrument Makers (*contd.*)

WIND GANES MADE AND MENDED BY WILLIAM BULL TRUMPETT MAKER TO HIS MAIESTIE WHO LIVETH *att the Sign of the Trumpett and Horne* IN CASTAL STREET NEARE THE MUYSE.' (See illustration p. 8.)

The Royal Mews stood on the site of The National Gallery, and 'was so called of the King's falcons there kept' (Stow).

'*At the Hautboy and 2 Flutes* IN BRIDE LANE COURT.'

'*At the Sign of the French Horn and Violin* OPPOSITE THE WAX WORK, FLEET STREET.'

'*At the Violin, Hautboy and German Flute* AT THE WEST END OF ST. PAUL'S CHURCHYARD.'

'MUSIC PRICKED.'

'JNO. JOHNSON AT *ye Harp and Crown,* CHEAPSIDE.' Dibdin the song writer was employed with this celebrated violin maker.

'HARPSICHORDS AND SQUARE PIANO FORTES.'

Musicians

'*Tabor and Pipe* IN HELMET COURT NEAR CATHERINE STREET, STRAND.'

'JOHN WARD *at the Violin and Hautboy* IN YE OLD CHANGE, CHEAPSIDE. PROVIDES MUSIC FOR CONSORTS, BALLS AND ASSEMBLIES.'

Mustard Maker

'BILL'S ORIGINAL DURHAM MUSTARD WAREHOUSE AT *The Fox* IN BUDGE ROW.'

Needle and Fish hook Makers

'W. WYLDE. NEEDLEMAKER TO HER MAJESTY AT THE *Queen's Arms* IN ST. PAUL'S CHURCHYARD.'

Nightmen

'ROBERT STONE, NIGHTMAN AND RUBBISH CARTER *at the Golden Pole,* THE UPPER END OF WHITE CROSS STREET. DECENTLY PERFORMS ALL HE UNDERTAKES. NOW CARRIED ON BY HIS DAUGHTER.' (Account on back dated 1761.)

Nightmen (*contd.*)

'WILLIAM LINGLEY, NIGHTMAN AND POLEMAN FOR THE CITY OF LONDON. NO. 35 IN THE OLD CHANGE, CHEAPSIDE.' (Dated 1774.)

Notary Public

Nurserymen

'PINE APPLES RAISED AND SOLD BY HENRY SCOTT, GARDENER AT WEYBRIDGE. HE HAS CUT RIPE PINE APPLES EVERY WEEK FOR 15 MONTHS PASSED AND SHALL CUT UNTILL YE LATTER END OF OCTOBER.' (Dated 1754.)

Note to illustration reads:

Explanation, 'KNOWLEDGE AND LABOUR (ASSISTED BY FOUR ELEMENTS) PRESENTING THE GARDENER WITH A CORNUCOPIA OF FRUITS.'

Oilmen

'THOS. WADDELL & SON, OIL AND COLOURMEN AT THE *Original Good Woman* NEAR St. GILES' CHURCH LONDON.' Larwood says the *Good Woman*, or *Silent Woman*, represents a headless woman and was particularly used by oilshops. He hazards a guess that it may have had some reference to the Heedless (Headless) or Foolish Virgins in the Parable.

'THE FINEST SALLET OYLS OR VIRGIN LUCA,' 'FLORENCE AND GENOA OYL FOR SCOWRING IRON OR BRASS,' 'OYL FOR PLAISTERS AND OYNTMENTS,' 'RAPE OYL FOR LAMPS,' 'MACKARONEE,' 'VERMAJELLY,' 'SALT PETER AND PETER SALT,' 'SALT PRUNELLA,' 'CHINA SOYE AND KETCHUP,' 'CAVEAR AND PICKLED OYSTERS,' 'MORRELLS AND TRUFFLES,' 'BOLOGNIA SAUSAGES,' 'SPRUCE BEER AND PEARL ASHES,' 'LEMON AND VERJUYCE,' 'LINKS AND FLAMBEAUX,' 'LAM-BLACK CORD AND PACK-THREAD.'

Paper Stainer

'AT THE CHINEE PAPER WAREHOUSE IN NEWGATE ST.'

Patten Makers

Pavior

Peruke Makers   'THOMAS BOWMAN, PERRUQUES INVENTED 1796 PATENT OBTAINED 1800.'

'MAKES ALL PERUKES AND LADY'S TATES IN THE NEATEST MANNER. LADIES BRAIDS AND CRAPE CUSHIONS.'

'*At the Sign of the Phoenix and Locks of Hair.*'

Pewterer   'PEWTER DISHES AND PLATES. ALEHOUSE POTS AND WINE MEASURES, TEAPOTS, PEWTER, OCCUMY AND WHITE METAL SPOONS, BELLOWS, BOX IRONS AND FLAT IRONS, CANDLESTICKS AND SNUFFERS. MAKES ALL SORTS OF PEWTER TOYS.'

'*At the Golden Dish* IN PATERNOSTER ROW NEXT CHEAPSIDE.'

Pin makers   'PIN MAKERS AND CITTIZENS ON LONDON BRIDGE.' (See Plate LXXVII.)

Pinkers

Pipe-makers

Plaster of Paris
Figure-maker

Poleman and Carter   'DECENTLY PERFORMS ALL HE UNDERTAKES.'

Pork-butcher   'SAUSAGES AND HOGS PUDDING OF A PECULIAR FLAVOUR.'

Potter   'JOSIAH WEDGWOOD, POTTER TO HER MAJESTY, BURSLEM IN STAFFORDSHIRE.'

N.B.—HIS MANUFACTURE IS SOLD AT HIS WAREHOUSE IN GT. NEWPORT ST., LONDON AND AT NO OTHER PLACE IN TOWN AND AS HE SELLS FOR READY MONEY ONLY HE DELIVERS THE GOODS SAFE AND CARRIAGE FREE TO LONDON.

Press-maker and Turner   'MAKERS OF WOODEN SCREWS FOR PRESSES.'

Printsellers

'DOROTHY MERCIER *at the Golden Ball* IN WIND-MILL ST. SELLS FLOWER PIECES IN WATER COLOURS PAINTED BY HERSELF FROM THE LIFE. AND FANNS FOR LADIES IN A NEW AND ELEGANT MANNER.' (See Plate LXXVIII.)

'ELIZABETH BAKEWELL MAP AND PRINTSELLER AGAINST THE END OF BIRCHIN LANE IN CORNHILL.'

'GLASS PAINTINGS AND PICTURES FOR CHIMNEY PIECES. MAKES ALL SORTS OF FRAMES IN THE NEATEST MANNER. STAIRCASES AND ROOMS NEATLY FITTED UP WITH INDIAN PICTURES AND ALL SORTS OF LIQUID COLOURS FOR SURVEYORS, ETC.'

'*At the Sign of Ye Laughing Painter* IN CROSS COURT.'

Prize Fighter

'JAMES FIGG, MASTER OF YE NOBLE SCIENCE OF DEFENCE. ON YE RIGHT HAND IN OXFORD ROAD NEAR ADAM AND EVE COURT. TEACHES GENTLEMEN YE USE OF YE SMALL BACK-SWORD AND QUARTERSTAFF.' (Engraved by Wm. Hogarth.)

Pump Maker and Pipe Borer

'FRANCIS SUTTON, SOHOO SQUARE. MAKES AND MINDS ALL SORTS OF WOODEN PUMPS. UNDER-TAKETH THE DIGGING AND CLEANING OF WELLS.'

Quack Doctors

'ELDRIDGE THE NORWICH ARTIST. THE TRUE PREPARER OF FRIAR'S GRAND ORIGINAL SPECIFIC BALSAM OF HEALTH; FINE PURGING SUGAR CAKES FOR WORMS; BENGAMOTT AND FINE CEPHALIC HERB-SNUFF FOR THE HEAD AND EYES.' (See also Plate LXXXVIII.)

Quill and Pen-makers

Ratcatcher and Sow Gelder

Razor Makers

At the Halbert.
At the Pistol and C. (See Plate LXXXI.)
At the Pistol and L.
At the E.T. and Crown.
At the Red M. and Dagger. (Compare under Cutlers). Also see p. 16.

Rocking-horse
  Maker

Scale Makers

'*At the Sine of the Porrige Pot* ON LONDON BRIDGE . . . . BEAMS STILLARDS & GOLD SCALES.'

'THE STANDARD W$^{tt\cdot}$ OF YE FOLLOWING COINS:

	DWT.	GR.
A JACOBUS	6	6
$\frac{1}{2}$ JACOBUS	3	3
CAROLUS	5	18
$\frac{1}{2}$ CAROLUS	2	21
GUINEA	5	9
$\frac{1}{2}$ GUINEA	2	$16\frac{1}{2}$
MOIDER	6	$22\frac{1}{4}$
$\frac{1}{2}$ MOIDER	3	11
PISTOL	4	8
$\frac{1}{2}$ PISTOL	2	4

NOTE THAT EACH GRAIN IN GOLD IS 2^d. AT $\frac{1}{4}$ P. OUN.' (See Plate LXXXII.)

Sedan Chair Maker

(See Plate LXXXIII.)

Sergeants at Mace

Shampooing Surgeon

'SAKE DEEN MAHOMET. THE ART OF SHAMPOO-ING FIRST INTRODUCED INTO ENGLAND BY HIM IN 1784.'

Shell Fish Warehouse

'*At the Oyster Girl* NO. 13 CHARLES STREET, SOHO SQUARE, DINNERS DREST AT THE SHORTEST NOTICE. MORNING, EVENING AND SUNDAY PAPERS IN THE COFFEE ROOM, GENTEEL ROOMS FOR THE RECEPTION OF COMPANY. BEST NATIVE OYSTERS WAR-RANTED GOOD BARRELLED.'

Ship Broker	'SELLS SHIPS OR PARTS OF SHIPS BY PUBLICK OR PRIVATE SALE. LETS SHIPS TO FREIGHT, ENTERS OR CLEARS SHIPS AT THE CUSTOM HOUSE.' (See Plate LXXXV.)
Ship-masters	'*The Henry and ffrancis.* ROBERT OSBORN MASTER IS NOW LOADING AT THE CUSTOM HOUSE KEY.'
Shot Maker	
Shoemaker	BLOOMFIELD, NO. 14 GREAT BELL ALLEY, COLEMAN ST. [The Poet-Shoemaker 1766-1823. Robert Bloomfield, author of 'The Farmer's Boy.']
Silk Thrower	
Skeleton Seller	
Skinner	'DEALER IN PHIALS.'
Smith	'MAKETH THE NEW INVENTED SMOAK JACKS WHICH ARE GREAT PREVENTERS OF CHIMNEYS SMOAKING.'
Snuff Dealers	'THE *Rasp and Crown.* FRIBOURG & TREYER N°. 34 UPPER END OF Yᵉ HAY MARKET.'
	'JOHN SAULLÉ & PONTET AT THE *Crown and Rasp,* SUCCESSORS TO THE LATE Mʳ. JAMES FRIBOURG, IN PALL MALL NEAR THE HAY MARKET. FRENCH MANUFACTURERS OF RAPEE SNUFF READY RASP'D OR UNRASPED.' (1768.)
	'RAPPEE AND STRASBOURG SNUFFS.'
	'FINEST BATTLE POWDER AT 1S. 6d. PER POUND.'
Spadderdash and Gaiter Maker	'JOHN DRAKEFORD *at the* 3 *Spatterdashes* NEAR EXETER CHANGE IN THE STRAND, MAKES AND SELLS ALL MANNER OF SPRING SPATTERDASHES.'
Stage Waggons and Coaches	'FLY VANS—LONDON TO CHELTENHAM IN 20 HOURS.'

Stationers — 'CIPHERING BOOKS, COPPY BOOKS, SLATES, SLATE PENS, POPE JOAN BOARDS, BACKGAMMON BOARDS, WAX WAFERS, SAND BOXES.'

Surgeon — 'SERVED KING CHARLES YE 2ND IN YE DUTCH WARRS.' (See Plate LXXXVIII.)

Sworn Brokers

Tailors — 'KERSEY BEAVER SURTOUTS,' 'SHAG BREECHES,' 'FINE JEAN AND NANKEEN HABITS,' 'RICH SATTIN FLORENTINE WAISTCOATS.'

W. COURT, TAILOR AND BREECHES MAKER, 17 GREAT PULTENEY S^t·, GOLDEN SQUARE. Adopts the device of Adam and Eve sewing fig leaves together.

Tambour Maker

Tea Men — 'AS THE ATTENTION IN TRADE IS HERE CONFINED TO THIS SINGLE ARTICLE A PREFERENCE THEREBY IS PLEADED AND THE CURIOUS IN TEA MAY DEPEND UPON HAVING IT CHEAP AND GENUINE, NOT AFFECTED IN TASTE OR SMELL BY MANY DISAGREEABLE ARTICLES KEPT BY TEA DEALERS.'
'GERMAN SPAW AND PYRMONT WATERS.'
'HUNGAREY AND LAVENDER WATERS.'
'VINELLO AND PLAIN CHOCOLATE.'
At the China Man and Tea Tree.

Ticket Porter

Tobacconist — '*At the Jessamine Tree,* HAVANNA AND PORTUGAL SNUFF.'
Brunn's Card—Tobacconist, of Great Marlborough St., portrays three men with this legend:
'THESE THREE UNITE IN ONE CAUSE,
THIS SNUFFS, THAT SMOAKES, THE OTHER CHAWS.'
The Snuffer says 'VOULEZ VOUS DE RAPE.'
The Smoker ,, 'NO DIS BEEN BETTER.'
The Chawer ,, 'WILL YE HA' A QUID.'

Tobacconist (*contd.*)

On the back is a bill

'lb.   £ s. d.

8 OF FINE TOBACCO AT 16ᵈ· PER POUND   o 10 8

lb.

8 OF MIDDLING „ AT 14ᵈ· „ „   o 9 4.'

'POOLES BEST VIRGINIA *at the too Golding Potts and Bottles* IN BRIDGE ST. COVENT GARDEN.'

Toymen   See Pewterers.

Trunk Makers

'VALEESES FOR BEDDING, PANNIERS, ENGLISH MAILS, HAIR PORTMANTUA TRUNKS, PERRI-WIG BOXES, CLOATH CLOAK BAGGS, FIRE BUCKETS AND BLACK JACKS, GAMBADOES FOR SEA AND LAND.'

'ALL SORTS OF TRUNKS FOR PLATE CHINA AND GLASS.'

'HAIR TRUNKS, SUMPTER TRUNKS, PORTMANTUA TRUNKS, GILDED LEATHER TRUNKS AND PERUKE BOXES, CANTEENS TO HOLD LIC-QUORS, CASES FOR PLATE, POST CHAISES AND ALL SORTS.'

Turtle Shell Worker   'NEW DISCOVERED TURTLE SHELL.'

Turners   'TURNER AND TOYMEN.'

'PATENT SPUNGE MAKER FOR GREAT GUNS AND TURNER TO THE HONOURABLE BOARD OF ORDNANCE, THE ROYAL NAVY AND THE HONBLE. UNITED EAST INDIA COMPANY.'

Umbrella Makers

'OIL'D SILK AND LAWN UMBRELLAS.

NEW INVENTED LONG TUBED UMBRELLAS.

LIKEWISE FOR THE GOUT, RHEUMATISM AND DROPSY KNEECAPS, ELBOW DO. BOOTIKINS, GLOVES, ETC.'

Undertakers

'YOU MAY BE FURNISHED WITH ALL SORTS AND SIZES OF COFFINS AND SHROUDS READY MADE AND ALL OTHER CONVENIENCES BELONGING TO FUNERALS.'

Undertakers (*contd.*)	'SAFETY FOR THE DEAD. SIR WILLIAM SCOTT HAS DECIDED THE RIGHT TO INTER IN IRON.'
	'FUNERALS DECENTLY PERFORMED.'
	'VELVET PALLS, HANGINGS FOR ROOMS, LARGE SILVER'D CANDLESTICK AND SCONCES, TAPERS FOR WAX LIGHTS, HERALDRY FEATHERS AND VELVETS, FINE CLOTH CLOAKS AND MIDLING DO. RICH SILK SCARVES, ALLAMODE AND SARSNETT HAT BANDS, BURYING CRAPES OF ALL SORTS.'
	'IMPROVED COFFINS—THE FASTENINGS OF THESE IMPROVED RECEPTACLES BEING ON SUCH A PRINCIPLE AS TO RENDER IT IMPRACTICABLE FOR THE GRAVE ROBBERS TO OPEN THEM. THIS SECURITY MUST AFFORD GREAT CONSOLATION AT AN ÆRA WHEN IT IS A WELL-AUTHENTICATED FACT THAT NEARLY ONE THOUSAND BODIES ARE ANNUALLY APPROPRIATED FOR THE PURPOSE OF DISSECTION.'
Upholsterers	'FOUR POST TENT BEDSTEADS WITH MORINE, HARATEEN, CHENEY AND CHECK FURNITURE.'
	'SOPHAS.'
	'ORGANS, HARPSICHORDS AND PIANO FORTES. N.B. DEALER IN COALS.'
Wax and Tallow Chandlers	AT THE '*Bee Hive and Wax Chandler.*'
	'MOULD AND STORE CANDLES. ALSO THE FINE AND TRUE SPERMA CŒTI CANDLES,' 'FRENCH DIAPHANE CANDLES,' 'FLAMBEAUX.'
Weaver	*At the Peacock.*
Whalebone and Cane Merchants	
Wire Drawer	'GOLD & SILVER WYER DRAWER AT THE *Shipp & Anchor* IN LOMBARD-STREET, NEARE GRACIOUS-STREET.'
Woad Dyer	'TO THE HON: EAST INDIA COMPANY.'
Wool Staplers	

CHAPTER VII

TRADE CARDS BY WILLIAM HOGARTH

FROM various sources I have compiled a list of Tradesmen's Cards by, or attributed to, William Hogarth. That all of these are authentic is doubtful. It is more than probable that some are the work of W. H. Ireland—son of Samuel Ireland the engraver—forger of the Shakespeare manuscripts, and were ascribed by him to Hogarth.

The greater number of those mentioned will be found in Austin Dobson's *Hogarth*; others are given in *Graphic Illustrations of Hogarth*, by S. Ireland; *Hogarth's Works,* by John Ireland and Nicholls; *Hogarth Illustrated*, by John Ireland; and in auction sales catalogues of the collections belonging to Mrs. Hogarth and S. Ireland. The portfolios in the Print Room of the British Museum contain examples of nearly all the engravings listed.

BOXER — JAMES FIGG, Oxford Road, near Adam and Eve Court. (Size $6\frac{1}{2}'' \times 4\frac{3}{4}''$.)
Will Hogarth fecit 1794.

BUN BAKER — RICHARD HAND, *King's Arms,* at Chelsey (see Plate V). (Size $7'' \times 5\frac{1}{4}''$.)
Wm. Hogarth, 1718 (?).

BUNN HOUSE — DAVID LOUDON's, at Chelsey (see Plate VI). Wm. Hogarth. (Size $14\frac{3}{8}'' \times 8\frac{1}{8}''$.)

DRUGGIST — JAMES BARTLETT, at *The Three Angels* in Cornhill. (Size $6'' \times 4''$.)
The plate is engraved $\frac{J.B.}{1720}$.
A bill on the back of the card is dated 28 April, 1725.

ENGRAVER — W. HOGARTH (see Plate XXX). (Size $4'' \times 2\frac{3}{4}''$.)
The plate is engraved 'Aprill ye 23.1720'. Samuel Ireland, in *Graphic Illustrations of Hogarth,* says: 'Hogarth's own shop or message card which bears the date April 21st 1720.' Said to be Hogarth's earliest work.

ENGRAVER (*contd.*) W. Hogarth at *ye Golden Ball,* ye corner of Cranborne Alley, little Newport Street.

W. Hogarth, delt. S.I.ft. (Size 4″ × 2¾″.)

The plate is engraved 'April ye 29 (?) 1720.' The day of the month is indistinct on all impressions I have seen. See also under Land Surveyor (p. 66).

ENGRAVERS' Solsull. Hogarth del. S.I. fect. 1781. PUNCH MAKER (Size 5½″ × 4½″.)

FAN MAKER Gordon. *Ye Golden Fan and Crown* in Tavistock St., Covent Garden. (Size 7″ × 5½″.)

W. Hogarth Invt. J. Sympson sculp.

An original drawing. I have seen no engraving.

FROCK SHOP Mary and Ann Hogarth. *Ye Kings Arms* joyning to ye Little Britain Gate. (Size 6¼″ × 4⅛″.)

Hogarth del. T. Cook sculp. (see Plate XXXIV).

In Samuel Ireland's *Graphic Illustrations* the plate is engraved 'W. Hogarth del J.I. fe'. Other impressions are without the names of artist or engraver. (Size 4⅛″ × 3⅝″.)

GOLDSMITHS Ellis Gamble (i) At *The Golden Angel,* in Cranbourn St., Leicester Fields. (Size 7⅜″ × 5¾″.)

   A. M. Ireland sculp. (see Plate XXXV).

   (ii) 'A contracted copy of above' (Ireland and Nicholls' *Hogarth's Works*).

   (iii) 'Arms of Ellis Gamble, a direction card.' W. Hogarth S.I. fect. (S. Ireland's *Graphic Illustrations*.)

GOLDSMITHS
(*contd.*)

JNO. MONTGOMERY *at the Angel,* corner of Cambridge St. in Golden Square. (Size $7\frac{3}{8}'' \times 5\frac{3}{4}''$.)

This is a replica of Ellis Gamble's card (i) above with the name and address suitably altered.

PETER DE LA FONTAINE, *at the Golden Cup* in Litchfield St. Soho. (Size $7\frac{1}{2}'' \times 6''$.)

W. Hogarth Ft. 1798.

Probably engraved by Sympson. (See Frontispiece.)

WILLM. HARDY in Ratcliff highway near Sun Tavern Fields. (Size $2\frac{5}{8}'' \times 2''$.)

A mutilated copy of this card was given to S. Ireland by Mr. Bonneau—no perfect impression has been found.

JOHN BARKER, *Morocco Ambassador's Head,* Lombard St. (Size $3\frac{7}{8}'' \times 2\frac{1}{2}''$.)

INN

RAM INN, Cirencester. (Size $4\frac{3}{4}'' \times 5\frac{1}{2}''$.)

W. H. fecit 1719.

JAMES SMITH (? *The Angel*), Barkway, Hertfordshire. (Size $3\frac{1}{4}'' \times 2\frac{3}{4}''$.)

The sign resembles Ellis Gamble's.

ITALIAN
WAREHOUSEMEN

MRS. HOLT, at *Ye Two Olive Posts* in ye Broad part of the Strand. (Size $6\frac{3}{4}'' \times 5''$.)

Hogarth del. A.M.I. fct. (see Plate XLIX).

JOHN MARCHI, at *The Three Jars and Two Flasks,* near the Little Theatre in the Haymarket. [No. 12 Haymarket.] (Size $7\frac{1}{4}'' \times 5''$.)

A replica of Mrs. Holt's card above. Dated 1772.

KILGOUR & CUMINE, New Bond Street. (Size $6\frac{1}{4}'' \times 5''$.)

The engraving of Mrs. Holt's card has been reversed and details slightly altered.

LAND SURVEYOR
AND ENGRAVER
J. CHAPMAN, Royal Academy, Pall Mall. (Size $2\frac{3}{4}'' \times 2\frac{1}{8}''$.) This engraving is an adaptation from Hogarth's card issued from *The Golden Ball*.

PAVIOR
'Sign for a Pavior.' (Size $4\frac{3}{4}'' \times 4\frac{3}{4}''$.) Hogarth pinxt. J.I. sculp., dated 1790. This is a design for a signboard rather than for a Trade Card.

SIGN PAINTER
'Design for a Shop Bill.' (Size $6\frac{5}{8}'' \times 5\frac{1}{8}''$.) Hogarth pinxt. Merigot sculp., dated 1799.

TOBACCONISTS
RICHARD LEE, at *the Golden Tobacco Roll* in Panton Street, Leicester Fields. (Size $4'' \times 3\frac{3}{8}''$.) W. Hogarth invt.

Compare Hogarth's *Modern Midnight Conversation.*

LACROIX'S, the Corner of Warwick Street, near Swallow Street, St. James's. (Size $2\frac{3}{4}'' \times 2\frac{1}{8}''$.) See illustration below.

HARRISON. A Tobacco paper.

UPHOLSTERER
(Name panel left blank.) (Size $8'' \times 7''$.) On the back is written 'Engraved by W. Hogarth 1731 in Fleet Street.'

A Tobacconist's Card by W. Hogarth

CHAPTER VIII

DESCRIPTIONS OF PLATES

With Notes on the Signs and Topography. Giving sizes, dates, and other particulars.

Except where otherwise mentioned, the examples are taken from the author's own collection.

Plate No.   GOLDSMITH

Frontispiece PETER DE LA FONTAINE *At the Golden Cup* in Litchfield Street, Soho, by William Hogarth. In Banks' Collection, dated 1798. (Size $7\frac{1}{2}'' \times 6''$.)

The Golden Cup was a sign derived from the arms of the Goldsmiths' Company and often used by Goldsmiths and Booksellers.

Litchfield Street ran from Upper St. Martin's Lane to Charing Cross Road. It is said that at No. 3 (Lady Paulet's) was a room with a ceiling which might have been painted by Hogarth.

The costumes are those of 1730-40.

BOOKSELLERS

I. JOHN WILKIE *At the Bible* in St. Paul's Churchyard, engraved by Corbould and Jeffreys. (Size $8'' \times 6''$.)

The Bible became the symbol of the Booksellers and Publishers at the Reformation. John Wilkie was at this address from 1757 to 1770, and published *The London Chronicle* there. Treasurer of the Stationers' Company. He died 1785. The house was afterwards numbered 71. It stood by the north door behind the Chapter House.

II. J. SEAGO. Print and Bookseller, High Street, St. Giles's. In the Banks Collection. Dated 1782. (Size $3\frac{1}{2}'' \times 2\frac{3}{8}''$.)

There is another card of J. Seago's, in which his address is given as 'High Street, St. Giles's near the Church' and embellished with an old ragamuffin in a tattered hat who is labelled 'Old Simon.' In this—probably earlier—card, he describes himself as Print-seller only.

BRAZIER

III. THOMAS PICKETT *At the Sign of ye Frying Pan* in Compton
   Street, Soho. (Size 6½″ × 3¾″.)
   'Citizen and Brazier' is written on the face.

   The sign bears the City Arms and another coat which
   is not discernible.

BREECHES MAKER

IV. JAMES POTTER *At the Sign of the Boot and Breeches,* in
   Shoemaker Row, Aldgate. (Size 6½″ × 3½″.)

   The makers of leather breeches for riding frequently
   combined their occupation with that of glover or
   bootmaker.

BUN BAKERS

V. RICHARD HAND *At the Kings Arms* at Chelsey, by Wm.
   Hogarth, dated 1718. (Size 7″ × 5¼″.)

   The ascription to Hogarth is a very doubtful one.

   The Royal Arms are those of George I. This celebrated
   Royal Bun House was kept by the Hand family for
   four generations. In Smith's *Book for a Rainy Day* is
   quoted an advertisement of Mrs. Hand, who kept the
   shop from 1738 to 1798, informing her customers that
   she had determined not to sell Hot Cross Buns on
   Good Friday—only Chelsea Buns.

VI. *David Loudon's Bunn House at Chelsey,* by Wm. Hogarth.
   In Mr. C. W. F. Goss's Collection. (Size 14¾″ × 8⅛″.)

   In the earlier impressions of this plate the name W.
   Hogarth does not appear—it was added later.

   Masonic emblems and costume. Arms of George I.
   Costume 1730 *circa.*

   It seems likely that this Bun-house is the same as that
   previously kept by the Hand family (see above).

   The building stood at the corner of Grosvenor Row

Plate No.   BUN BAKERS (*contd.*)

(now 60 Pimlico Road), and contained a Museum of Curiosities, amongst which were two lead figures, 4 ft. high, of British Grenadiers (see figures in illustration). A good description and a drawing appears in Beaver's *Memorials of Old Chelsea*. It was pulled down in 1839.

CABINET MAKERS

VII. CHARLES BLYDE *At the Chair and Tea Chest* in Knaves Acre. (Size 8″ × 6″.)

'Knave's Acre or Pulteney Street, Golden Square . . . . . chiefly inhabited by those that deal in old goods and glass bottles'—Strype.

VIII. JOHN BROWN *At the Three Cover'd Chairs and Walnut Tree,* St. Paul's Churchyard. (Size $7\frac{1}{2}$″ × 5″.)

On the back of this card is an account dated 1738 for 'a large corner cabinet 15/-.' The Walnut Tree was a sign often adopted by cabinet makers. On the south side of St. Paul's Churchyard there was a Tavern of this name, and an eighteenth-century engraving shows a large tree on that side.

John Brown was here from 1728 to 1744. His shop was at the East end of the Churchyard near the school.

CALICO PRINTER

IX. JACOB STAMPE *At ye Sighn of the Callico Printer* in Hounsditch. (Size $5\frac{7}{8}$″ × 5″.)

In the Bagford Collection.

A very early example of the woodcut Trade Card. Green, in his *History of the English People*, mentions this card as being *temp.* James II.

Houndsditch—formerly the City Ditch surrounding the wall from the Tower to the Fleet by Newgate.

CARPENTER

X. Henry Sidgier *At the Carpenters Arms* in Great Shere Lane (Temple Bar). (Size 6½″ × 5″.)

The Arms are those of the Carpenters' Company. 'Sheer Lane, or more properly Shire Lane, so called because it divideth the Cittie from the Shire'—(Stow). It had an unenviable reputation, and the name was changed to Lower Serle's Place. It was finally cleared away at the building of the Law Courts.

CHEMIST

XI. Richard Siddall *at the Golden Head* in Panton Street, Haymarket. R. Clee fecit. (Size 10″ × 7″.)

The Head is possibly that of Glauber, a very favourite sign with Chemists. Another example of this card in the Banks Collection is dated 1781. An illustration of it appears in Hodgkin's *Rariora*. A similar card in the Hon. Gerald Ponsonby Collection bears the names Siddall & Swann.

CHIMNEY SWEEP

XII. George Cordwell *at the Golden Broom,* Grosvenor's Mews, near Berkley Square. (Size 7½″ × 4¾″.)

In the Banks Collection. Dated 1784.

The Royal Arms are those of George II.

CHINA AND GLASS SELLERS

XIII. Jane Taylor & Son *at the Feathers* in Pall Mall. (Size 6″ × 4¾″.)

The small panels below the sign show a Tea Merchant and a Glass Blower's furnace.

Pall Mall is said by Wheatley to have been the first London street lighted by gas in 1807.

Plate No. ### CLOCK MAKER

XIV. Math^w· Gaucheron *at the Dial* in Tower St., near ye
7 Dials. J^n· Fougeron, Sculp^t· (Size 7″ × 5″.)

Where the seven streets met in St. Giles in the Fields
stood a column, erected in 1694 and removed in 1773.
In Evelyn's *Diary,* and again in Gay's *Trivia,* this is
described as bearing seven dials, but Thorne, in his
Handbook to the Environs of London, 1876, says that the
block on which the dials were fixed is distinctly six-
sided and is used as a mounting block near 'The
Ship Inn,' Weybridge. The column itself was re-
erected on Weybridge Green in 1822.

CLOG MAKER

XV. Thos. Berry *At the Patten and Crowne,* under St.
Dunstan's Church in Fleet Street. (Size $6\frac{1}{4}$″ × $4\frac{1}{4}$″.)

In the Banks Collection. Dated 1799.

This beautifully drawn card is reproduced in Hodgkin's
Rariora.

CLOTHIERS

XVI. Casaltine & Mathews '*At the Lamb and Star* the
2^d shop in Houndsditch, faceing Aldgate Church.'
(Size 8″ × 5″.)

Houndsditch (see under Plate IX).

XVII. Kenelm Dawson *At the Sign of the Jolly Sailor* in Monmouth Street (St. Giles'). (Size $5\frac{1}{2}$″ × 4″.)

Monmouth Street in the eighteenth century was noted
for its second-hand clothiers' or 'slop shops.'

Costume 1740 *circa.*

COALMAN

XVIII. John Edwards '*At the Old Collier and Cart* at Fleet Ditch
near Holborn Bridge.' (Size 4″ × $3\frac{1}{2}$″.)

This card has a space at the bottom for the account.

Plate No.   COALMAN (*contd.*)

The specimen referred to contains an invoice dated
1717 for
            '1 Load of Coals & all Accounts 17/-.'

'The Fleet Ditch' was cleaned out, enlarged and banked
in 1670 to allow of the passage of barges up as far as
Holborn.   The Fleet joined the Old Bourne at the
foot of Holborn Hill.

COLOURMAN

XIX.   NATHAN DRAKE *At the White Hart,* Long Acre.   In the
Franks Collection.   (Size 7″ × 5½″.)

The White Hart couchant with collar and chain was the
ordinary badge of King Richard II, surnamed
of Bordeaux.

Long Acre has been noted for its famous coach-makers
since the seventeenth century, and no doubt attracted
ancillary trades such as those of Colourmen.

CONFECTIONER

XX.   D. NEGRI *At the Pine Apple* in Berkeley Square.   (Size
7½″ × 6½″.)

The Pineapple was the emblem generally adopted by
confectioners in the eighteenth century.

Negri and Gunter were confectioners at the '*Pot and
Pineapple*, Berkley Square,' in 1784.

In the Banks Collection is a card of Negri and Wetten
at Berkeley Square and also of Wetten and Son,
19 Bruton Street, dated 1785 and 1801.

In the same collection is a card of 'Gunter, confectioner,
31 New Bond Street, from Mr. Negri's.'   This is
dated 1787.

No. 5 Berkeley Square has long been famous in its
connection with Messrs. Gunter.   The building of
the Square itself was begun in 1698.

Plate No.   COPPER PLATE MAKER

XXI. Benjamin Whittow *At the Crown in Shoe Lane* (Holborn). (Size 7¼" × 6".)

The Crown is one of the oldest signs, and is read of as early as 1467. Shoe Lane was a centre for Sign Painters and the designers of broad-sheets.

COSTUMIER

XXII. Jackson's Habit Warehouse in Tavistock Street, Covent Garden. Woodifield sculp^t·

In Mr. E. E. Newton's Collection. Dated 1770.

Tavistock Street in the eighteenth century was one of the most fashionable shopping streets.

CUPPER

XXIII. John Rigg. 'At the Hummums in the Little Piazza, Covent Garden.' Woodifield, Sculp^t· (Size 7" × 5½".)

'Hummums is a Bagnio or place for sweating in Covent Garden. Here is also a cold bath for such as are disposed to use it.'—Hatton's *New View of London,* 1708.

John Rigg states that 'it has always been kept and preserved for near an Hundred Years.'

CUTLER

XXIV. John Brailsford, 'in ye Broad part of St. Martins Court, Leicester Fields.' (Size 6" × 4".)

On the back of this card various prescriptions have been noted, one is headed 'Receipt for ye Jaundies.'

DAIRYMAN

XXV. Thos. Edwards *at the Ass and Foal,* Marylebone Lane. (Size 7" × 6".)

In the Banks Collection. Dated 1781.

　　　　　DENTIST

XXVI. Law. No. 10 St. Albans Street, Pall Mall. (Size 4″ × 3″.)
In the Banks Collection. Machy, sculpt.

DRAWING MASTER

XXVII. T. Sandby, Junr. St. George's Row, Oxford Street.
(Size 9½″ × 6½″.)

B. West, R.A., inv: F. Bartolozzi, R.A., etched.

Published May, 1791, by T. Sandby, Junr., St. George's
Row.

B. West was elected P.R.A. in the following year.

The address is the same as on that of the card of Paul
Sandby the artist. A proof before letters is in the
Franks Collection.

DYER

XXVIII. John Wildblood *at the Rainbow and 3 Pidgons* in St.
Clements Lane in Lombard Street. (Size 5½″ × 3¾″.)

In the Victoria and Albert Museum.

The Rainbow was a favourite and appropriate sign for
Dyers, and this device, not dissimilarly drawn, is to be
seen on the poster of a Dyer and Cleaner to-day.

ENGRAVERS

XXIX. Wm. and Cluer Dicey *at the Maidenhead* in Bow Church
Yard. (Size 8″ × 6″.)

'It is impossible to determine whether "the Maiden-
head" was set up as a compliment to the Duke of
Buckingham, to Catherine Parr, or to the Mercers'
Company, for it is the crest of the three . . . . but
since Elizabeth's reign it has doubtless frequently
referred to the Virgin Queen.' (Larwood and Hotten's
History of Signboards.) It was a sign used by the early
printers.

Plate No.   ENGRAVERS (*contd.*)

In *The London Journal,* 1724, is an advertisement of Cluer's Printing Offices, and a later one gives notice that the business is carried on by his widow, Elizabeth Cluer.

The firm seems always to have specialised in the engraving of Shopkeepers' Bills, and in one advertisement adds, 'Likewise Mr. Handel's Operas are there Engraved, Printed and Sold.'

XXX. W. HOGARTH, dated Aprill ye 23. 1720. (Size 4″ × 2¾″.)

In the Franks Collection.

Bryan's *Dictionary of Painters and Engravers* says that this card is Hogarth's earliest known work. It appears in S. Ireland's *Graphic Illustrations of Hogarth.*

See list of Hogarth's Trade Cards on p. 63 and also Plate V, which it will be seen is dated 1718. A somewhat similar card bears the wording:

'W. Hogarth
Engraver at *ye Golden Ball*
Ye corner of Cranbourne Alley
Little Newport Street.'

In the Sale Catalogue of Samuel Ireland's Collection this is described as Hogarth's 'shop-bill or message card.'

FIRE ENGINE MAKER

XXXI. JOHN BRISTOW. Ratcliffe Highway, Larken sculpt. Dated 1775. (Size 9½″ × 6″.)

The Manual Engine is marked 'J. Bristow fecit.'

The three badges below it are those of The London Assurance, The Sun, and The Royal Exchange Fire Insurance Companies. In the Guildhall Library is another card of John Bristow with 'A Perspective View of part of the Ruins of the late dreadful Fire which happened in Cornhill March 25th, 1748.' This one has the badges of twenty-one Fire Insurance Companies.

Plate No.   FRAME MAKERS

XXXII. Ross. No. 113 Gt. Portland Street. Pergolesi del. et
     sculpt.   (Size 3″×5″.)

   In the Banks Collection. Dated 1788.

XXXIII. Joseph Cox in Round Court in St. Martin's-le-Grand.
     (Size 6″×3¾″.) In the Banks Collection. Dated 1786.

FROCK SHOP

XXXIV. Mary and Ann Hogarth. 'From the old Frock Shop
     the corner of the Long Walk facing the Cloysters.
     Removed to *Yᵉ King's Arms* joyning to yᵉ Little
     Britain Gate near Long Walk.' (Size 6¾″×4¾″, also
     4⅛″×3⅝″.)

   Hogarth del: T. Cook sculpt.

   This engraving is usually considered to be one of the
     Ireland forgeries.

   Mary and Ann were sisters of Wm. Hogarth who died
     1764. Mary, born 1699, predeceased her brother, and
     Ann, born 1701, died in 1771. Little Britain is said,
     according to Stow, to have taken its name from a
     mansion used by the Dukes of Brittany. It was
     famous for its Booksellers' Shops.

   The Cloisters, those of Christ's Hospital, adjoined Long
     Walk and led to St. Bartholomew's Hospital; the
     Gate was one leading into Christ's Hospital.

   The costumes shown are 1730-1740.

GOLDSMITHS

   De la Fontaine (see note to Frontispiece, p. 67).

XXXV. Ellis Gamble at *the Golden Angel* in Cranbourn St.,
     Leicester Fields. A. M. Ireland sculpt. (Size 7⅜″×5¾″.)

   Wheatley's *London Past and Present* quotes the following
     extract from Knowles' *Life of Fuseli:*

   'At the *Golden Angel* in Cranbourne St. Leicester Fields
     lived Ellis Gamble the goldsmith to whom Hogarth

Plate No. GOLDSMITHS (*contd.*)

was apprenticed to learn the art of silverplate engraving. [1712.] A shop-bill engraved for Gamble by this eminent apprentice is greatly coveted by the collectors of Hogarth's works and fine impressions fetch extraordinary prices.'

Samuel Ireland considered his own impression of this card to be unique—it is certainly very rare. In the Catalogue of the Sale of Ireland's Collection, 1797, it is recorded that this print had previously fetched £7.

Cranbourne Street or Alley (see description to Plate LXXXVI).

XXXVI. JOHN RAYMOND *at the Boy and Corall* in Gutter Lane. (Size 6″ × 4″.)

In the Franks Collection.

XXXVII. BENJAMIN CARTWRIGHT *At the Crown and Pearl,* near ye George Inn, West Smithfield. (Size 7½″ × 5½″.)

GROCERS

XXXVIII. GEORGE FARR *at the Bee-hive and Three Sugar Loaves* in Wood Street near Cheapside. (Size 9″ × 6¼″.)

The *Three Sugar Loaves* was the most usual sign for Grocers and Tea-men.

Wood Street, Stow suggests, was named after Thos. Wood (Sheriff 1491), but it was so called before that date. The well-known tree at the Cheapside corner marks the site of the church of St. Peter-in-Cheap.

A Spanish horse snuff mill and a Scotch mull are shown at the foot of this card.

XXXIX. RAY AND LUMLEY *At the Tea-Tub, Three Sugar Loaves and Crown* near Cruched-Fryers in Mark Lane. J. Watts, sculpt. (Size 6″ × 4½″.)

Mark Lane, or originally Mart Lane, 'so called of a privilege sometime enjoyed to keep a mart there.'

Plate No.   GROCERS (*contd.*)

Stow says, 'In this Street (Hart Street or Crutchet Friars) sometime Stood one house of Crouched (or Crossed) Friars—founded about the year 1298.'

The Great Fire broke out in Mark Lane (compare Pepys's *Diary,* Sep. 2, 1666).

XL. JOHN RICHARDSON '*At the CaniSter and Three Sugar Loaves* againSt Hatton Garden.' (Size $5\frac{1}{4}'' \times 4''$.)

On the back of this card is a bill dated 1756 which reads:
'A Single Loaf 10lbs. 13oz. at 8d.   0   7 $2\frac{1}{2}$
Souchong Tea   1lb.   0 10   0 '

HABERDASHERS

XLI. PEARSON 'at the *Royal Point* in TaviStock Street, Covent Garden.' Bride, sculpt. Dated 1774. (Size $8\frac{3}{4}'' \times 7''$.)
The sign denotes the Laceman.

This is a good example of the Trade Card which has a bill-heading printed on the back of it (see p. 2), where the full name (Matthew Pearson) is given, and the Street number (74) has been inserted.

An earlier card of Pearson's adds 'of Paulin's' to the address. Paulin's was a famous haberdasher, also in TaviStock Street (see p. 19).

XLII. SIBBELLA LLOYD, MARTHA WILLIAMS & ELIZABETH STOREY '*at Ye Three Angels* againSt George Yard, Lombard Street.' (Size $7\frac{1}{2}'' \times 5''$.)

Three Angels was a sign often adopted by Linen Drapers.

In R. Harwood's Plan (1792) this house is numbered 32 Lombard Street.

Hilton Price, in his *Signs of Lombard Street,* gives:
No. 32 *Three Angels,* 1723. Mary Browne and
                                               Margaret Morris.
              1731. Richard Browne.

Plate No.   HABERDASHERS (*contd.*)

The *George and Vulture* Inn mentioned in *The Pickwick Papers* stood at the end of George Yard.

XLIII. JAMES RAYNOLDS *At the Hand and Penn* in Rusell St., Covent Garden. (Size $5\frac{1}{4}'' \times 3\frac{3}{4}''$.)

The *Hand and Pen* was the Sign of Scriveners and Writing Masters.

HATTERS

XLIV. CHARLES PAGET *at the Black Boy and Hatt,* High Holbourn. (Size $8'' \times 5''$.)

XLV. THOMAS COLLYER '*at ye King's Armes and Beaver* in Exchange Alley in Cornhill.' (Size $7\frac{1}{2}'' \times 4\frac{1}{2}''$.)

'Haberdasher of Hatts.'

The origin of the word haberdasher, according to Skeat, is Icelandic—*hapurtask,* from the haversack in which pedlars carried their wares.

The Royal Arms are those of William III, 1689-1702, and it was no doubt out of compliment to him that the advertisement is repeated in Dutch. Exchange Alley now Change Alley.

HOSIERS

XLVI. WILLIAM ROBERTS '*at the Three Squirrils* in Jermyn Street.' (Size $5'' \times 6''$.)

'Cages with climbing squirrels and bells to them were formerly the indispensable appendages of the outside of a Tinman's shop, and were, in fact, the only live sign.' (Larwood and Hotten's *History of Signboards*.)

A bill made out by W. Roberts to Charles Howard, Esq. (afterwards the 11th Duke of Norfolk), is dated 1775. Gray the poet was in the habit of lodging at Robert's the hosiers at the east end of Jermyn Street.

XLVII. THOMAS MOORE '*à l'Enseigne de l'Evesque Blaze* dans Chiswell Street' (Finsbury Square). (Size $8'' \times 6\frac{1}{4}''$.)

Plate No.   HOSIERS (*contd.*)

Bishop Blaze or Blaize, otherwise St. Blasius, was Bishop of Sebaſte in Cappadocia, and became the patron saint of Woolcombers. He is represented with the inſtrument of his martyrdom—an iron comb.

The arms are those of George III.

In the Franks Collection is a rather similar card of Thomas Moore, but with the letterpress in English and without the Royal Arms. At the foot is a frame-knitting machine. On the back is a bill dated 1777. The plate is signed B. Webb script. Morrison sculpt.

INSTRUMENT MAKER

XLVIII. JAMES SIMONS '*at Sir Isaac Newton's Head* Marylebone Street.' (Size 6½″ × 4¾″.)

Longmate, sculpt.

Marylebone Street (Regent Street) was built *circa* 1680, and was so called because it led from Hedge Lane (now Whitcomb St.) to Marylebone.

ITALIAN WAREHOUSEMAN

XLIX. MRS. HOLT *at ye Two Olive Poſts,* Strand.

Hogarth del. A. M. Ireland sculpt. (Size 6¾″ × 5″.)

In the Catalogue of the Sale of Samuel Ireland's Collection it is ſtated that this print had previously sold for nine guineas.

This same design is used on the Billhead (dated 1772) of John Marchi at the *Three Jars and Two Flasks,* wine merchant, in the Haymarket. Slightly altered, it appears again on the Trade Card of Kilgour & Cumine, grocers, in New Bond Street.

The *Olive Tree* was a common sign for Italian Warehousemen.

Plate No.   LAMPLIGHTERS

  L. JOHN CLARK, Denmark Street, St. Giles-in-the-Fields.
(Size $6'' \times 7\frac{1}{2}''$.)

  LI. WILLM. CONAWAY, in Dean Street, Soho. (Size $5\frac{1}{2}'' \times 4''$.)
The card shows Monmouth House, Soho Square, built
by Sir Christopher Wren, where Bateman's Buildings
now stand. See details on p. 26.

The same engraving appears on the card in the Banks
Collection of Joel Iles, oilman, Queen Street, Soho.

LIBRARY

  LII. FRANCIS NOBLE's at '*Otway's Head,* King Street, Covent
Garden.' Ravenet, sculpt. (Size $7\frac{1}{2}'' \times 5\frac{1}{4}''$.)

Francis Noble died 1792.

The costumes date this card 1745-1750.

In 1770 there were only four Circulating Libraries in
London. The earliest was Wright's in the Strand,
started in 1740.

LINEN DRAPERS

  LIII. BENJAMIN COLE '*at the Sun* in St. Paul's Churchyard.'
B. Cole, sculpt. (Size $6'' \times 4''$.)

The costume is that of the reign of George I or late
Queen Anne, 1710-1720.

  LIV. JOHN MORRIS '*at the Old Black Boy* in Norton Folgate.'
(Size $5\frac{3}{4}'' \times 4''$.)

The *Black Boy* was usually a tobacconist's sign.

  LV. EDWARD EYRE '*at the Wheatsheaf* in York Street, Covent
Garden.' (Size $5\frac{3}{4}'' \times 3\frac{3}{4}''$.)

The *Wheatsheaf* is more commonly a baker's sign.

  LVI. PETER ORTON '*at the Black-Moors Head* in Fleet Street,'
dated 1754. (Size $7\frac{1}{4}'' \times 5''$.)

Negroes were called Black Moors or Black-a-moors to
distinguish them from the Moors or Tawny Moors.

  LVII. E. JEFFERYS '*at the Dolphin* over against Middle Row,
Holborn.' (Size $6'' \times 3\frac{3}{4}''$.)

Plate No.   Linen Drapers (*contd.*)

Middle Row was an island row of houses towards the south side of the street by Holborn Bars, nearly opposite the end of Gray's Inn Road. It was pulled down in 1867.

In the Hon. Gerald Ponsonby Collection there is a later card of Jefferys' with a Chippendale frame.

MERCERS

LVIII. Edward Nourse *at ye Turks Head*, Cheapside. (Size $6\frac{1}{2}'' \times 4\frac{1}{4}''$.)

This house was subsequently No. 13 Cheapside. It was occupied in 1744-1766 by Phipps & Henley, Mercers
1760   by John Henley, Mercer.
1767   by Edwards, Salmon & Ryder, Mercers.

LIX. Cranston '*at the Three Nuns and Wheatsheaf* in Great Bridge Street, Westminster.' (Size $8\frac{3}{4}'' \times 7\frac{3}{4}''$.)

The *Three Nuns* was a sign often adopted by drapers. The connection has been accounted for by the reputation that the holy sisterhoods had for being expert in lace embroidery and other fine work.

LX. Adams's '*at the Seven Stars* in Norris Street, near St. James's, Hay Market.' (Size $7'' \times 4\frac{3}{4}''$.)

The seven stars of the Pleiades is one of the Masonic emblems. Norris Street led westward from the Haymarket into St. James' Market, which last was demolished to make way for the southern part of Regent Street. In the centre stood a large Market Hall.

LXI. Wm. Ryder and Edwd. Nicklin *at the Indian Queen*, by the Cloisters, West Smithfield. (Size $7\frac{1}{4}'' \times 5''$.)

The Cloisters are St. Bartholomew's.

LXII. Whitehead Rumball '*at the Golden Anchor* near the New Church in the Strand.' (Size $6'' \times 4''$.)

Plate No.   MERCERS (*contd.*)

'The New Church' is St. Mary-le-Strand, built by
    James Gibbs in 1714. Here stood the great Maypole
    which was set up in 1661.

'What's not destroyed by Time's devouring hand
Where's Troy, and where's the Maypole in the
    Strand?'

Bramston, *Art of Politics*, 1731.

'Where the tall Maypole once o'erlooked the Strand.'

Pope, *The Dunciad.*

LXIII. EDWARD ARGLES *at ye Indian King*, near Warwick Court,
    Holborn.   (Size 7¼″ × 5″.)
Warwick Court stands on the site of the Earl of War-
    wick's house.

LXIV. GABRIEL DOUCE *'at ye Lamb and Black Spread Eagle'* in
    New Round Court, Strand. (Size 5¼″ × 4¼″.)
In the Franks Collection.
New Round Court was on the north side of the Strand
    where now stands the Charing Cross Hospital.

LXV. GARNHAM EDWARDS *'at the Old Indian Queen,* faceing
    Hatton Garden, Holborn.' (Size 5¾″ × 4¼″.)
The shop probably stood on the site of John Gerard's
    garden—his *Herbal* was published in 1597. On the
    other side of Holborn were the gardens of Hatton
    House.

MILLINER

LXVI. MARTHA WHEATLAND AND SISTER *'at Queen Charlott's
    Head,* Near Wood Street, Cheapside.'
W. Tringham, sculpt., dated 1761. (Size 7″ × 5¼″.)
The Queen of George III rarely figures on signs.

From the fourteenth to the seventeenth century only the
    shops of goldsmiths were permitted in Cheapside;
    after Charles I it was inhabited by mercers and
    linen drapers.

LXVII. WILLIAM WOODWARD, 1 Marylebone Passage, Wells
Street, Oxford Market. (Size $7\frac{3}{4}'' \times 6''$.)

In the Victoria and Albert Museum.

Oxford Market was demolished in 1880; the site is now
occupied by Oxford Mansions.

LXVIII. JOHN HUNT in Goswell Street, near Mount Mill. (Size
$7'' \times 5\frac{1}{2}''$.)

Mount Mill in Goswell Street (now Goswell Road) was
on the east side, opposite Compton Street.

PAPERSTAINER

LXIX. JAMES WHEELEY 'opposite the Church in Little Britain.'
(Size $6'' \times 7''$.)

In the Banks Collection.

The costume here indicates 1760 to 1770.

Little Britain, in early days 'Brettone Strete.' Stow
derives the name 'of the Dukes of Brittany lodging
there.'

PAPERSTAINER AND ENGRAVER

LXX. MATTS. DARLY '*At the Acorn* facing Hungerford,
Strand.' (Size $10'' \times 7\frac{3}{8}''$.)

Matt. Darly inv. & sculpt. In the Banks Collection,
dated 1791.

M. Darly was a well-known caricaturist, engraver and
printseller. A large number of the plates for
Chippendale's *The Gentleman and Cabinet-makers'
Director* (1754-1762) were engraved by him.

Charing Cross Station stands on the site of Hungerford
Market.

Plate No. PAWNBROKER

LXXI. JOHN FLUDE, No. 2 Grace Church Street.

Delegal sculpt. From Mr. E. E. Newton's Collection.

In Norden's Map of London, Gracechurch Street is marked 'Gratious Street.' Stow terms it 'Grasse Street.'

PERFUMER

LXXII. RICHARD WARREN '*at the Golden Fleece* in Mary-le-Bonne Street, Golden Square & fronting Wood Street, Cheapside.' (Size $6\frac{3}{4}'' \times 8\frac{1}{2}''$.)

New Complete Guide, 1777, gives Warren at Marylebone Street.

London Directory, 1784, places him at No. 5 Marylebone Street, and also at No. 41 Cheapside.

Marylebone Street (see description, Plate XLVIII).

PERUKE MAKERS

LXXIII. WILLIAM JOHNSON in Castle Alley, Royal Exchange.

Engraved by Grayhur.

Castle Alley now Castle Court. (Size $7'' \times 5\frac{3}{4}''$.)

Costume 1750 *circa.*

LXXIV. THOMAS GIBBONS '*at the Blew and White Peruke* in Rosemary Lane.' (Size $5\frac{1}{2}'' \times 4\frac{1}{4}''$.)

Rosemary Lane—now Royal Mint Street, formerly Hog Lane; here was a notorious mart for old clothes called the Rag Fair.

PEWTERERS

LXXV. THOS. SCATTERGOOD '*at the Blackmoors Head* near the South Sea House in Bishopsgate Street.' (Size $4\frac{3}{4}'' \times 3\frac{3}{4}''$.)

South Sea House, built for the famous company in 1711 —now the home of 'The Baltic.'

Thomas Scattergood was Warden of the Pewterers' Company in 1733; his 'touch' or mark was Two

Plate No. PEWTERERS (*contd.*)

Hands with Hammers and a Rose. His son, Thomas Scattergood, was Warden 1770 and 1773, and Master in 1774 and 1775.

Blackmoor's Head (see description notes to Plate LVI).

LXXVI. JOHN KENRICK, near Cherry Garden Stairs, Rotherhithe. (Size 6¾″ × 4¾″.)

In the Victoria and Albert Museum.

John Kenrick was Renter Warden of the Pewterers' Company in 1754. His 'touch' was a Stork.

PIN-MAKERS

LXXVII. GEORGE WORRALL, THO. WEAVER, JN. WOODWARD, and JN. JEFFERIS, dated 1756. (Size 6½″ × 4″.)

The Arms are those of the Pinners' and Needlers' Company.

Pennant says 'most of the houses on London Bridge were tenanted by Pin-makers. The houses were removed in 1761.' Most of them were demolished before that date—one tenement, that leased to Mary Russell and let to John Evans at the 'South East End,' stood until Lady Day, 1762.

Until the erection of Westminster Bridge in 1750, this was the only bridge over the Thames at London.

PRINTSELLER

LXXVIII. DOROTHY MERCIER '*at the Golden Ball* in Windmill Street, Golden Square.' (Size 10″ × 6″.)

In the Banks Collection, dated 1781.

The costumes are those of 1750-1760.

QUACK

LXXIX. DR. JAMES's POWDERS 'sold only by J. Newbery, *at the Bible and Sun* in St. Paul's Churchyard.' (Size 16″ × 10″.)

T. Kitchin sculpt. In the Banks Collection, dated 1782.

Bible and Sun, No. 65 St. Paul's Churchyard, was occupied in 1757-1775 by John Newbery, Publisher.

QUACK (*contd.*)

'Here Johnson sold the *Vicar of Wakefield* for 60 guineas for Oliver Goldsmith. . . . Newbery appears from old advertisements to have done a large business in patent medicines. . . . The site is now occupied by The Religious Tract Society.' (Hilton Price's 'Signs of Old London,' in *London Topographical Records,* Vol. III.)

John Newbery was the pioneer publisher of special books for children.

RAZOR MAKERS

LXXX. HENRY PATTEN '*at the Saw and Crown* in Middle Row, Holborn.' E. Warner sculpt. (Size $7\frac{1}{2}'' \times 6''$.)

Middle Row (see notes on Plate LVII).

LXXXI. JAMES BERNARDEAU '*at the Pistol and L.* in Russell Court, Drury Lane.'

Russell Court was a foot passage from Drury Lane to Catherine Street.

An initial was often introduced into cutlers' signs (see p. 16). The description is repeated in French.

SCALE MAKERS

LXXXIIA. JOHN PICARD '*at ye Hand and Scales* the corner of Maiden Lane in Wood Street.' (Size $3\frac{1}{2}'' \times 2\frac{1}{4}''$.)

John Picard is known to have been in business at this house in 1726.

LXXXIIB. TIM^hy· ROBERTS '*at the Hand and Scales* next ye Corner of Queen Street in Watling Street.' (Size $2\frac{3}{4}'' \times 1\frac{3}{4}''$.)

Queen Street was made just after the Great Fire to give a direct route from the Guildhall down to the river.

This card is interesting, as it gives the gold coinage of James I, together with the foreign gold pieces in currency.

Plate No.   SEDAN CHAIR MAKER

LXXXIII. W. INSLEY in Marylebone Street, St. James's. In the Banks Collection, dated 1780. (Size 5″ × 3½″.)

Sedan Chairs were introduced into England by the Duke of Buckingham in the reign of Charles I.

SCHOOLMISTRESS

LXXXIV. MRS. MASQUERIER'S, Church Lane, Kensington. In the Banks Collection, dated 1782. (Size 5½″ × 7″.)

SHIP BROKER

LXXXV. WILLIAM LEM, Exchange Alley. T. Kirk, sculpt.

In the Franks Collection. (Size 7¾″ × 6¼″.)

Thomas Kirk, painter and engraver, exhibited at the R.A., 1785-1796.

SHOEMAKER

LXXXVI. JOHN SNOWDON *'at the Angel and Three Shoes* in Cranbourn Alley.' (Size 6″ × 4″.)

Cranbourne Alley or Street was a paved footway from Castle Street to Leicester Square; it was famous for its milliners' shops.

On the back of this card is noted, 'The Bootmaker's Bill for a Paire of Boots for the Boy £0. 12. 6.' Dated 1764.

STATIONER

LXXXVII. DANIEL RICHARDS 'at St. Andrews Church, Holborn.' (Size 5½″ × 4″.)

St. Andrew's on Holborn Hill (see p. 27).

Daniel Richards born 1715, died 1802.

'Father of the Parish of St. Andrews. Kept a stationer's

Plate No.   STATIONER (*contd.*)

shop for 60 years. Senior member of the Court of Assistants of the Stationers' Company.'—('Timperly's *Printers' Manual.*)

He also issued another and rather later card, a simply lettered announcement enclosed in a 'Chippendale' frame.

SURGEON

LXXXVIII. CHARLES PETER, St. Martin's Lane. Ant. Schoonian pinxt. Jos. Nutting sculpt., dated 1705. (Size $8\frac{1}{2}'' \times 5\frac{3}{4}''$.)

Engraved British Portraits mentions this plate:

'Charles Peter Surgeon and Empiric   b. 1648'

Hodgkin reproduces this card in his *Rariora.*

Anthonie Schoonjans, b. 1650, d. 1726.

Joseph Nutting, famous engraver of portraits.

TALLOW CHANDLER

LXXXIX. THOMAS PAYNE 'in St. Ann's Lane near Aldersgate.' (Size $6'' \times 4''$.)

Stent fecit.

Displays the Arms of the Tallow Chandlers' Company.

In St. Ann's Lane, now Gresham Street, stood the church of St. Ann-in-the-Willows, destroyed in the Great Fire and rebuilt by Sir Christopher Wren.

TEA DEALER

XC. ROBERT FOGG '*at the China Jarr* in New Bond Street.' (Size $4\frac{1}{4}'' \times 3\frac{1}{8}''$.)

TINMAN

XCI. ROBERT HOWARD '*at the Wheatsheaf and Trumpet,* Smithfield Bars.' (Size $6\frac{1}{2}'' \times 5''$.)

This was the great grandfather of J. E. Hodgkin, collector and author of *Rariora.*

Plate No.   TRUNK MAKERS

XCII. SAMUEL FORSAITH '*at Industry and Indolence* in Long Acre.' Willm. Clark, sculpt. (Size 7¾″ × 6″.)

XCIII. JOHN CLEMENTS, 'the corner of St. Pauls next Cheapside.' (Size 7¾″ × 6″.)

Bill on back dated 1762.

Hilton Price's *Signs of Cheapside* gives *Bucket and Truck* No. 7 Cheapside, corner of St. Paul's Church-yard, occupied by Bundy. Portmanteau, leather fire buckets, hose truck makers. Probable date 1760.

TRUSS MAKER

XCIV. JOHN RICHARDSON '*at the Golden Key*, Prescot Street, Goodmans Fields.' (Size 5¾″ × 3½″.)

Hatton, in 1708, speaking of Prescott Street, said: 'Instead of Signs the houses here are distinguished by numbers as the staircases in the Inns of Court and Chancery.' This street is usually considered to be the first one in which numbering of houses was adopted.

On the back is a bill dated 1748, under which is written, 'If it Does not fitt please Return it and I will alter it or Change it.'

TURNER

XCV. ELIZ. BARTON STENT '*at the Turners Arms* in Little Britain.' (Size 6¾″ × 3¾″.)

Little Britain (see note to Plate LXIX).

UNDERTAKERS

XCVI. GEORGE SMITHSON '*opposite the Bull and Gate,* Holbourn,' dated 1740. (Size 6½″ × 5″.)

'Bull and Gate,' a corruption of Boulogne Gate, one of the gates of Calais.

Plate No. UNDERTAKERS (*contd.*)

XCVII. ROBERT GREEN '*at the Four Coffins,* St. Margaret's Hill, Southwark,' dated 1752. (Size 8″ × 6½″.)

The same engraving is found on the card of George Page, undertaker, at the same address.

UPHOLSTERERS

XCVIII. JAMES RODWELL '*at the Royal Bed and Star,* faceing Bedlam Walk in Moorfields.' (Size 8½″ × 6″.)

The 'Walk' alongside the Bethlehem Hospital was a fashionable promenade in the early half of the eighteenth century.

XCIX. ROBERT LEGG '*at the Sign of ye Leg*' in Holborn. (Size 7¾″ × 6″.)

M. Darly sculpt. (see note to Plate LXX).

Occasion was often taken to use a rebus in Tradesmen's signs, cards, and tokens. (See Larwood and Hotten, p. 469 *et seq.*)

WOOLLEN DRAPERS

C. PETER HODGSON '*at the Wool Pack* in Grace Church Street.' (Size 6¼″ × 5¼″.)

Gracechurch Street (see note to Plate LXXI).

CI. RICHD. FAWSON '*at the Golden Fleece,* St. Paul's Churchyard.' (Size 7¾″ × 6″.)

T. Kirk sculpt. (see note to Plate LXXXV).

DIVINITY

Law

Physick

Poetry

History

Mathematicks

Shakespear

Clarke

Milton

Boyle

Locke

Wollaston

Dryden

Newton

Addison

Whitby

Pope

John Wilkie

BOOKSELLER (and **PUBLISHER**,

At the Bible, late Mr. Rich.d Baldwin's

near the Chapter-house, in St. Paul's Church Yard,

London.

Sells Books in all Languages & Faculties.

Bibl's, Common Prayers & School-books

of all Sorts, Wholesale or Retale.

Periodical Publications of all kinds.

Play Cards, Pocket Cases of the newest

fashion, & Stationary Wares of all Sorts.

NB. Ready Money for any Library

or Parcell   of Books.

Stationary

Tillotson

Young

all Sorts of   Wares

Bibles   School-books   Testaments

I

J. Seago,
Print &
BOOKSELLER.
High Street,
S.ᵗ GILES'S,
near Tottenham
Court Road.

Prints, Drawings, & Books bought.

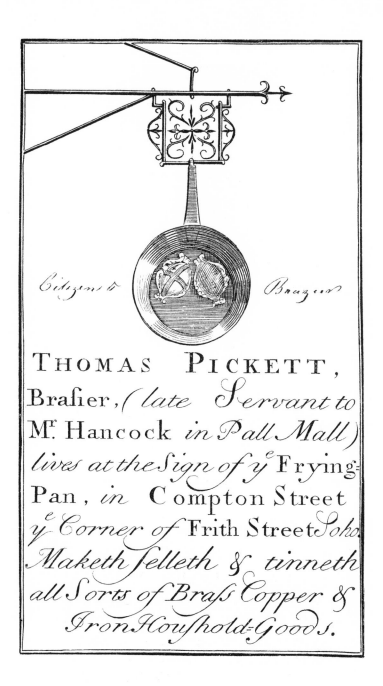

Citizen & Brazier

THOMAS PICKETT, Braſier, (late Servant to Mr. Hancock in Pall Mall) lives at the Sign of ye Frying=Pan, in Compton Street ye Corner of Frith Street Soho. Maketh ſelleth & tinneth all Sorts of Braſs Copper & Iron Houſhold=Goods.

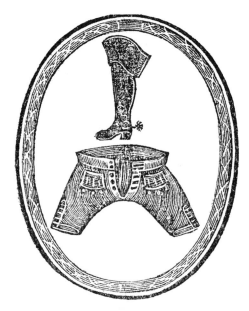

James Potter,

Leather - Breeches   Maker.

At the Sign of the Boot *and* Breeches,
within Three Doors *of* Aldgate, *on
the* Left Hand Side *of the* Way, *in*
Shoemaker-Row.

Maketh and Selleth all Sorts of
Leather-Breeches, by Whole-
fale and Retail, at Reafonable Rates.
Likewife Buck and Doe Skins and
all Sorts of Leather for Breeches.

Printed at the Old Katherine-Wheel without Bifhopfgate.

IV

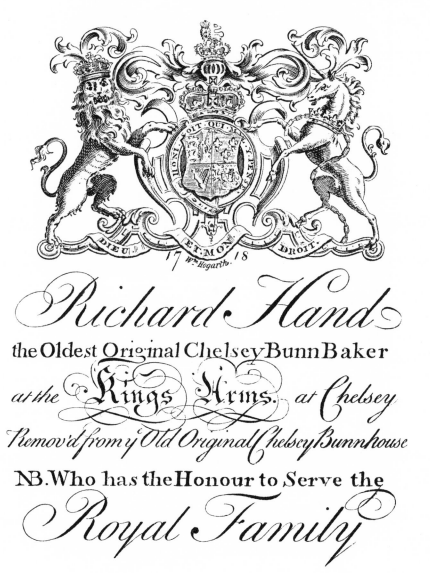

Richard Hand

the Oldest Original Chelsey Bunn Baker

at the Kings Arms, at Chelsey

Remov'd from y Old Original Chelsey Bunnhouse

NB. Who has the Honour to Serve the

Royal Family

A Perspective View of David Loudon's Bunn House At Chelsey Who Has the Honour to Serve the Royal Family.

Wm Hogarth

VI

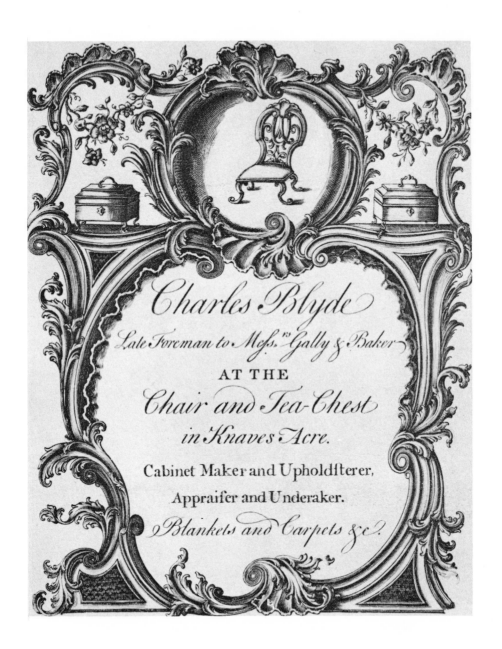

Charles Blyde

Late Foreman to Mess.rs Gally & Baker

AT THE

Chair and Tea-Chest

in Knaves Acre.

Cabinet Maker and Upholdſterer,

Appraiſer and Underaker.

Blankets and Carpets &c.

VII

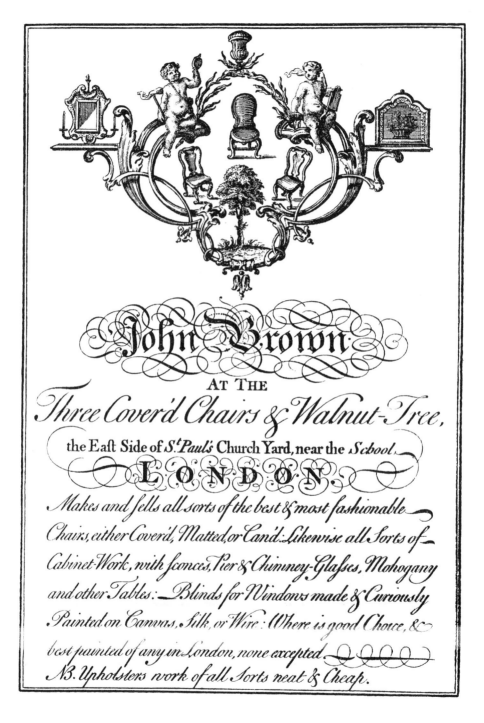

John Brown

AT THE

Three Cover'd Chairs & Walnut-Tree,

the Eaſt Side of S.ᵗ *Paul's* Church Yard, near the *School*

L O N D O N

Makes and ſells all ſorts of the beſt & moſt faſhionable
Chairs, either Cover'd, Matted, or Can'd: Likewiſe all Sorts of
Cabinet-Work, with ſconces, Pier & Chimney-Glaſses, Mohogany
and other Tables: Blinds for Windows made & Curiously
Painted on Canvas, Silk, or Wire: Where is good Choice, &
beſt painted of any in London, none excepted
N.B. Upholſters work of all Sorts neat & Cheap.

VIII

Jacob Stampe living at ij Sighn of the Callico
Printer in Hounsditch Prints all sorts of
Callicoes Lineings Silkes Stuffs
New or Ould at Reasonable Rates

IX

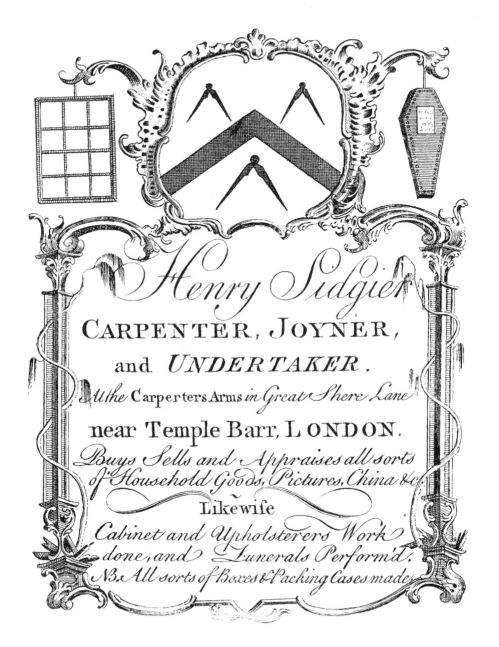

Henry Sidgier

CARPENTER, JOYNER,

and *UNDERTAKER*.

At the Carpenters Arms in Great Shere Lane

near Temple Barr, LONDON.

*Buys Sells and Appraises all sorts
of Household Goods, Pictures, China &c*

Likewise

*Cabinet and Upholsterers Work
done, and Funerals Perform'd.
NB. All sorts of Boxes & Packing Cases made.*

x

Richard Siddall

Chymist,

at the Golden Head in Panton Street,

near the HAY-MARKET,

Makes and Sells all manner of

Chymical and Galenical Medicines,

With all Sorts of Druggs;

Wholesale & Retail at very Reasonable Rates.

N.B. The Elixir for the Asthma, as also
for the Gout and Rheumatism.

George Cordwell,
CHIMNEY-SWEEPER to their
Royal-Highness's the Duke's of
-GLOUCESTER and CUMBERLAND.
at the Golden Broom, the Top of Grosvenor's Mews, near
Berkley Square. Extinguishes Chimneys
when on fire, fixes and Cleans Coppers and
Smoak Jacks, Cures Smoaking Chimneys in
Town or Country (no Cure no Pay) and by
strict Attention to Business Himself,
performs what He undertakes with the
utmost care and expedition.

XII

ICH DIEN

Jane Taylor & Son
China and Glass Sellers
to his Royal Highness ij Prince of Wales,
At the Feathers in Pall Mall,
London.
Sell all sorts of China Ware, Cutt and
Plain Glass, Finest Teas & Chocolate
Wholesale & Retail.

Math.w Gaucheron,
Successor to Mr Vitu,
CLOCK and WATCH-MAKER
at the Dial in Tower Street near ye 7 Dials
LONDON
NB Sells all sorts of Clock & Watch Makers
Goldsmiths & Jewellers Tools & Materials

Math.w Gaucheron,
Successeur de Mr Vitu
HORLEGEUR
Au Cadran dans Tower Street proche
——— des 7 Cadrans Londres ———
NB Vendent toutes Sortes d'Outils
& Materiaux Pour les
Horlogeurs Orfevere
Jouailliers

Jn Fougeron Sc

XIV

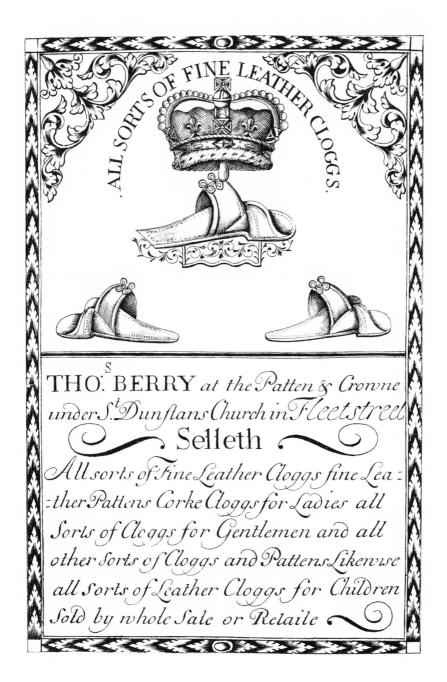

ALL SORTS OF FINE LEATHER CLOGGS.

THO.ˢ BERRY *at the Patten & Crowne under Sᵗ Dunstans Church in Fleetstreet* Selleth

All sorts of Fine Leather Cloggs fine Leather Pattens Corke Cloggs for Ladies all Sorts of Cloggs for Gentlemen and all other Sorts of Cloggs and Pattens Likewise all Sorts of Leather Cloggs for Children Sold by whole Sale or Retaile

Casaltine & Mathews

At the Lamb and Star the 2.ᵈ Shop in
Houndſditch Faceing Aldgate Church
LONDON.

*Sell all Sorts of Mens and Boys Cloaths
Ready Made, Likewise Cloths, Drugets, German-
Serges, Sagathies, Durvys, Fustians, Shaggs, Dimi
tys and Shalloons in the Piece, Mens Morning-
Gowns, Banyans, Cloth Cloaks, Riding Hoods,
Riding Habits, Quilted Coats, Hoop-Petticoats
Childrens Coats, as Likewise Stuffs, Camblets, Calla
mancos, Damasks, Norwich Crapes, Burdets &c,
in y Piece, Wholesale & Retail at Reasonabe Rates.*

Kenelm Danson

S A L E S M A N

at the Sign of the Jolly Sailor, in Monmouth Street,

L O N D O N.

Makes & Sells all sorts of Men & Boys Cloaths, of Cloth
Drugget German Serges & Fustians Cuttifull & Fashionable Morn-
-ing Gowns, Rocklors, Great Coats &c Likewise Buys and Sells,
all Sorts of Second hand Cloaths, both Rich & Plain. If any
Person have any to Dispose on, Please to send to my House, &
I will wait on them, and Give to the Utmost Value
Gentlemen may have great Choice of Cloaths &c in the Piece
where they may Chuse their Colours have Suits and Liveries
made at Reasonable Rates

A T *the* Old Collier *and* Cart,
at Fleet-Ditch, *near* Hol-
born-Bridge, *Are good Coals,
Deals, Wainſcote and Beach,* &c.
ſold at reaſonable Rates, by
John Edwards.

Nathan Drake

COLOURMAN.

Successor to

Mr. Robert Keating

At the WHITE HART in LONG-ACRE;

London.

Sells all sorts of fine Colours & Oils for painting
Prym'd Cloths, stencils fine Tools and Palletts;
Water Colours prepared in the neatest manner
Also Makes all sorts of Crayons in the best
Approved methods. Likewise Lines cleans and
mends Pictures and has every Article that is used
—— in Painting or Drawing. ——
all sorts of Colours & Oils for House Painting
at the Lowest Rates ——
(NB: Keatings fine Varnish formerly Call'd
Coopers Picture Varnish, so much
Approv.d of by Gentlemen for
Varnishing Pictures

XIX

Benjamin Whitow
Copper and Brass Plate
MAKER
At the Crown in Shoe Lane,
opposite the White Swan near St Andrew's Church,
HOLBORN
London
Makes Plates for Engravers,
Painters, Callico Printers. &c.
Country Orders, duly Executed.

Jackson's Habit-Warehouse
in Tavistock Street Covent Garden,
are to be Let.
A very Large Sortment of Character and other
Masquerade Dresses,
Particularly Rich Venetian Dominos, Trim'd and
Embellish'd in a Taste intirely New, with the
New Invented Silk-Masks.

NB. All sorts of Dresses made in the most Genteel & best manner,
And in order that the Nobility and Gentry may not be at a loss,
how to make choice of any particular Dress, may see a Book of
several Hundred prints Coloured, which Contains the Dresses
of every Nation.

XXII

John Rigg
CUPPER,
At the
Hummums in the Little Piazza Covent-Garden,
With a Back Door from Charles Street
Where GENTLEMEN only
May be always Accommodated (if not full)
in the best and neatest manner with
Lodging, Sweating, Bathing, or Cupping,
And with the utmost Decorum, as
has always been Kept and preserv'd for
near an Hundred Years.

Likewise
Ladies are Permitted only
to Sweating, Bathing, and Cupping,
With great Care & Proper Attendance.
N.B. Gentlemen or Ladies who desire to be
Cupped at their own Houses either in Town
or Country, shall be waited on
There is likewise a good Cold Bath.

Woodifield in Maiden Lane Sculp

XXIII

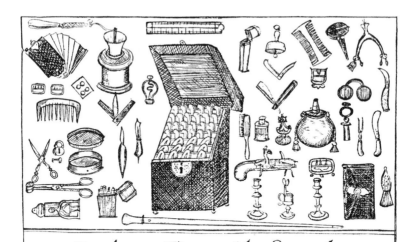

John Brailsford

CUTLER *in y Broad part of St = Martins Court* LEICESTER FIELDS *maketh &* Selleth *all Sorts of the Best* LONDON Work *Knives Forks* Razors *Scissors Penknives fleams Gardners & Painters Knives Fine Steel &* Met=tle *Buckels, Cork Screws Spurs Snuffers* Tobacco *& Snuff* Boxes *Powder Horns Dogs Collers &* Pad=locks *Ivory Box & horn Combs* Ivory *Pocket* Books *& Brushes Canes Rules Pencils Curl*ling Tongs Ink Stands *&c with all Sorts of Birmingham & Sheffield* Ware *& Fitteth up Silver China & Aggett Hafts wth y best Steel* Blades *at Reasonable Rates.* Canes Mounted

XXIV

ASSES MILK SOLD

Asses Bought & Sold or lett to Milk,
in TOWN *or* COUNTRY *by Tho.ᵘ Edwards,*
(Grandson to the late Mꝛ Abraham Eastey)
at the Afs & Foal, the bottom of Wigmore Street, in
Marylebone Lane, near Cavendish Square.

NB. Gentlemen & Ladies serv'd at any hour
of the Day.

XXV

DIEU ET MON DROIT

LAW,
Dentist,
N.º 10 St Albans Street,
PALL-MALL.
Pupil of the late M.ᶜRae,
Surgeon Dentist to His Majesty,
and His Royal Highness
the Prince of Wales.
FAMILIES,
attended by the Year

ICH DIEN

XXVI

XXVII

Iohn Wildblood at the Rainbow &
3 pidgons in St Clements Lane
In Lombard Street London who
Married the Widdow Harrinton
Silk Dyer

XXVIII

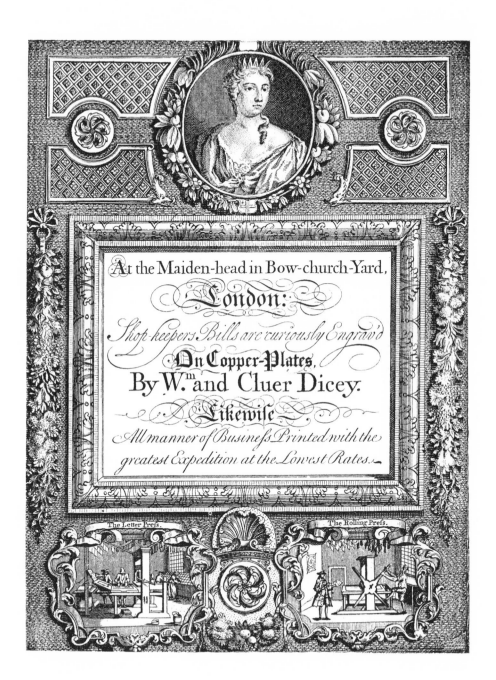

At the Maiden-head in Bow-church-Yard,
London:
Shop-keepers Bills are curiously Engrav'd
On Copper-Plates,
By W.ᵐ and Cluer Dicey.
Likewise
All manner of Business Printed with the
greatest Expedition at the Lowest Rates.

The Letter Press.   The Rolling Press.

XXIX

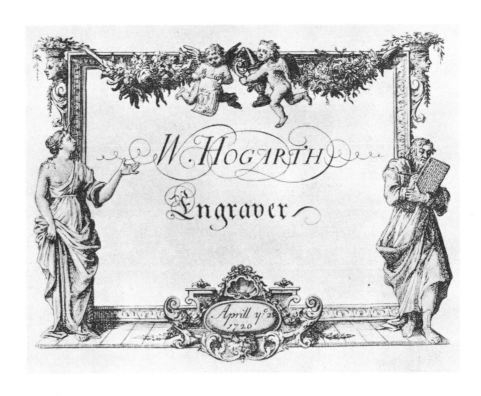

W. Hogarth
Engraver

Aprill y.e 25
1720

xxx

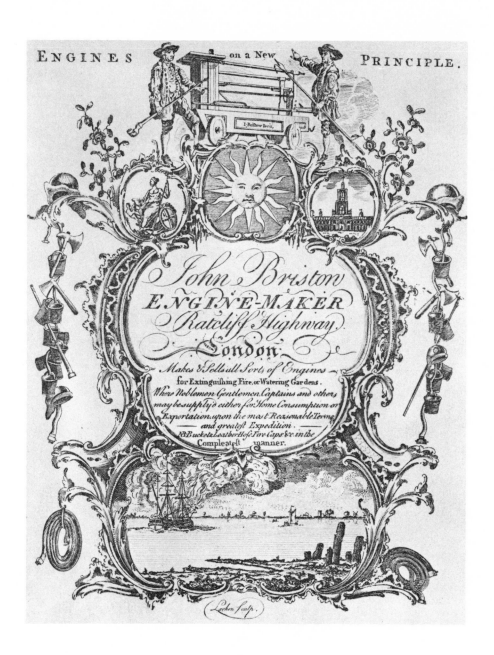

J. Bristow fecit.

John Briston

ENGINE-MAKER

Ratcliff Highway,

London.

Makes & Sells all Sorts of Engines
for Extinguishing Fire, or Watering Gardens.
Where Noblemen Gentlemen. Captains and others
may be supply'd either for Home Consumption or
Exportation, upon the most Reasonable Terms
and greatest Expedition.
N.B. Buckets, Leather Hose, Fire Caps &c. in the
Compleatest manner.

Larken Sculp.

XXXI

CHIMNEY PIECES

Ross
JOINER, CARVER, GILDER
& PICTURE FRAME MAKER,
At his Composition Ornament
MANUFACTORY,
N.º 113 Great Portland Street,
PORTLAND CHAPEL

Pugolss del.t   et Sculp.t

XXXII

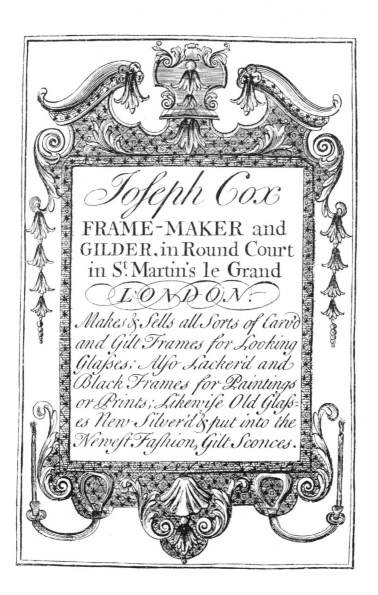

Joseph Cox

FRAME-MAKER and
GILDER, in Round Court
in St. Martin's le Grand

LONDON.

Makes & Sells all Sorts of Carv'd
and Gilt Frames for Looking
Glasses: Also Lacker'd and
Black Frames for Paintings
or Prints; Likewise Old Glass-
es New Silver'd & put into the
Newest Fashion, Gilt Sconces.

XXXIII

Hogarth del.   T. Cooke sculp.

Mary & Ann Hogarth

from the old Frock-shop the corner of the
Long Walk facing the Cloysters, Removed
to ye Kings Arms joyning to ye Little Britain-
gate near Long Walk Sells ye best & most Fashi-
onable Ready Made Frocks, sutes of Fustian,
Ticken & Holland, stript Dimmity & Flanel
Wastcoats, blue & canvas Frocks & bluecoat Boys Dra,
Likewise Fustians, Tickens, Hollands, white
stript Dimitys. white & stript Flanels in ye piece,
by Wholesale or Retale, at Reasonable Rates.

XXXIV

Ellis Gamble

GOLDSMITH,

at the Golden Angel in
Cranbourn-Street,
LEICESTER-FIELDS.

Makes, Buys & Sells all
sorts of Plate, Rings, &
Jewells, &c.

Ellis Gamble

ORFEURE,

a L'Enseigne de l'Ange d'Or
dans Cranbourn-Street
LEICESTER-FIELDS

Fait, Achete, & Vend toutes
sortes d'Argenterie, Bagues,
& Bijouxs, &c.

XXXV

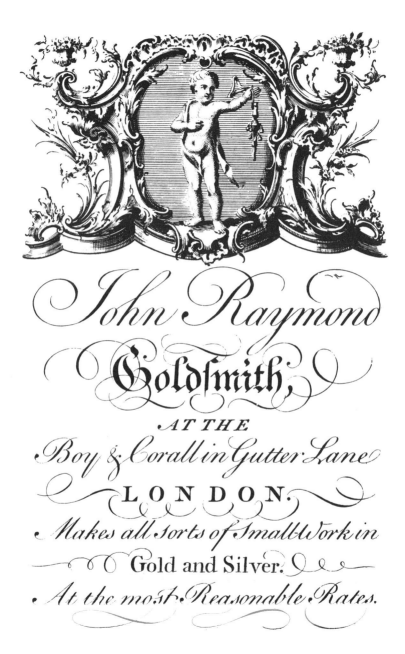

John Raymond

Goldsmith,

AT THE

Boy & Corall in Gutter Lane

L O N D O N.

Makes all sorts of Small Work in

Gold and Silver.

At the most Reasonable Rates.

XXXVI

Benjamin Cartwright
WORKING·GOLD·SMITH
at the Crown & Pearl near ye
George Inn, West Smithfield
London.

Makes & sells at ye lowest Prices, all sorts of Large
& small Plate, both wrought & plain, Rings and all
manner of Jewellers Work, also makes & mends
Watches. — NB. The Utmost Value given
for Sec.d hand
Plate, Watches,
Rings, old Gold and
Silver Lace.

XXXVII

George Farr
GROCER.
At the Bee-hive and Three Sugar Loaves
in Wood Street near Cheapside
London.
Sells all Sorts of Fine Teas, Coffee,
Chocolate, Sago Best Spanish, Scotch, Rappee
and Portugal Snuffs, Finest Blues & Starch,
with all others Grocerys.
Fine Old Rum, Coniac Brandy,
Batavia Arrack neat as Imported,
at the Lowest Prices.

Ray and Lumley
Grocers and Confectioners
At the Tea-Tub,
three Sugar-Loaves, and Crown,
near Crucbed-Fryers, in Mark-Lane,
London;
(from Mr. Rawlinsons, in Fencburcb-Street,)
Sell Fine Teas, Coffee, Chocolate, Cocoa Nutts, &
Snuffs, Sago, Hartshorne, Virmichelly, Morells,
Truffles, Starch & Blue, with the best of all Sorts of
Grocery, and Confectionary Wares,
at the lowest Prices.

J. Watts Sculp.

John Richardson

Grocer.

at the Canister and three Sugar Loaves

agaiſt Hatton Garden Holborn

London.

Sells Fine Teas, Coffee, Chocolate, Snuffs, Sago,
Hartshorn, Vermichelly, Starch, Stone & Powder Blues
With all sorts of Grocery & Confectionary Wares.
Wholeſale and Retail.

The ROYAL POINT

PEARSON,

Warehouse-Man, *HABERDASHER*, & Habit Maker,

at the Royal Point, in Tavistock-Street, Covent-Garden, LONDON.

Sells, Wholesale & Retail: Mignonnett, Brussels, Point, Blond and Black

Laces:

Kersemeres.......	Work'd Muslin Ruffles	Chip & Straw Ditto....	Leather Gloves & Mittens...
Sup.r Fine Thin Cloths....	Handk.s & Aprons......	Silk & Gauze Handkerchiefs...	Sattin & Lustring Ditto....
Allapeens, Fustains....	Bath Flannel Coats.....	All sort of Fashionable Ribbons	Patent Silk D.o....
Indianets and.......	Marseilles Quilting for..	Water'd & Plain Ditto......	All Sorts of Pins & Needles..
Dimities........,..	Bed Gowns & Coats.....	Flower'd Strip'd & plain Gauzes	Threads Tapes & Cottons..
Sup.r Fine Rattens....	French Hoops &c......	Italian White Crapes......	All sorts of Lisle Threads &c..
D.o Duffels....	Rich Flower'd & plain Sattin	Black Ditto........	Silk & Thread Purses...
with all sorts of Gold..	& Sarsenets for Cloaks &c...	Italian Gauzes......	Gold & Silver Ditto....
& Silver Trimmings....	All Sorts of Cardinals & Cloaks	Blond & Thread Trolleys...	Silk Lacing......
Hats & Feathers....	Plain Strip'd & Flower'd Muslin	India & French Fans....	Ladies Silk, Thread &..
Sattin, Sarsenet & Persian	Ladies Wrapping Gowns	Feather Muffs & Tippets...	Cotton Stockings....
Quilted Petticoats....	Gentlemens Morning Ditto	Fur D.o & Trimmings....	Jet Stomachers and..
All sort of Stuff D.o..	All sorts of Fashionable..	Italian & French Flowers...	Sleeve Knots &c.
Callico D.o & Bed Gowns.	Hats & Bonnets......	Fancy'd Stomachers & Tippets	

For Ladies Riding Dresses.

And all other Sorts of Haberdashery & Millenery Goods, which the Fashions produce

N.B. Ladies Brunswick, & all other Dresses Made, Likewise Huzars for Young Gentlemen.

Sibbella Lloyd Martha Williams & Elizabeth Storey
at ỹ three Angels against George Yard, Lombard street,
LONDON.

Sells all sorts of Baskets, Pincushions, Chimney Lines,
Blankets, Rollers, Mantles, Cradles, & Linings, Bed Chairs &
Tables, Childrens Dimity Coats, Holland Frocks, Flannel Petty
coats, Stockings & Shoes, Quilted, & Bed Gowns Wastcoats and
Holland half Shifts, Sattin & Callicoe quilted Bed Quilts,
Toilots for Tables, Damask & Diaper Clouting Hollands &
Callicoes, India & French Quilting, Dimitys strip'd & figur'd,
best Bone & Cane Hoops, Sattin, Sarcenet, Persian, Callicoe
Russel, & Callimanco Quilted Pettycoats, Velvet and Silk
Scarves, Manteels, Mantilets Pilgrims & Hoods, silk, scar-
let & light colour'd Cloth Cloaks, double & colour'd Velvets
of all sorts.

N.B. Likewise Makes & Sells all sorts of Riding Dresses,
Widows Weeds, Mens morning Gowns & Bannyans Vests &
Tunicks, Jocky Caps silk & Leghorn Hatts.

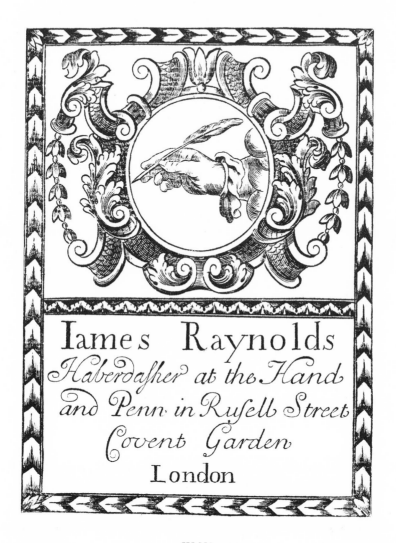

Iames Raynolds
*Haberdasher at the Hand
and Penn in Ruſell Street
Covent Garden*
London

XLIII

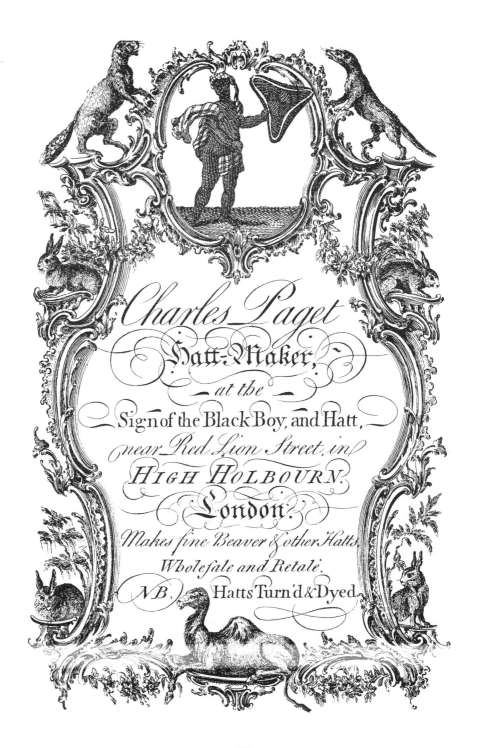

Charles Paget
Hatt-Maker,
at the
Sign of the Black Boy, and Hatt,
near Red Lion Street, in
HIGH HOLBOURN.
London.
Makes fine Beaver & other Hatts
Wholesale and Retale.
NB. Hatts Turn'd & Dyed.

IE MAIN: TIENDRAY

*Thomas Collyer Haberdasher of Hatts
at y̆ Kings Armes & Beaver in Exchange
Alley in Cornhill* London.

*Thomas Collyer Merchand Chapelier
aux Armes du Roy et Castor dans Exchange
Alleé dans Cornhill* A LONDRES.

Thomas Collyer Hoet Verkooper int.
Wapen van Englandt een Bever in de
Exchange Alley in Cornhill LONDON.

William Roberts
Hosier, Hatter, & Haberdasher,
at the three Squirrils in Jermyn Street,

London.

Sells all sorts of Hats Silk, Thread
Cotton & Worsted Hose, Silk & Worsted Pieces,
for Waistcoats, & Breeches, Likewise Hats,
& Hose, made of any Size or Pattern
at the Lowest Prices.

XLVI

G^m   R.

Thomas Moore,
Marchand fabricant de Bas & Bonneterie
De la Majesté Britanique
Demeurant à l'Enseigne de l'Evesque Blaze dans Chiswell Street
à LONDRES

Fait & Vend, tant pour le dehors que pour la consomption du Royaume,
toutes sortes de Bas de Soije, de Coton, fil & Laine tant tricottés que faits au metier,
Comme aussi des pieçes faites au metier pour Vestes & culottes de toute espece,
de même que toutes sortes de Bourses, Gans & Mitaines, de Coton, fil, Soije, & Laine, &c.
Il vend aussi, toutes sortes de Matériaux pour fabriquer les articles cy dessus
Specifiés.

Il est le premier en Angleterre qui a entrepris de faire la
Tapisserie Royale veloutée à la Persienne, qu'il a porté
à un grand degré de perfection en Tapis, Ecrans, dos & Sieges
de Chaises &c". de toute beauté & à bon marché.

XLVII

Mathematical Philosophical & Optical Instruments, are accurately made according to the Best & Latest Improvements, by JAMES SIMONS, At Sir Isaac Newton's Head, the Corner of Marylebone Street opposite Glasshouse Street London.

XLVIII

AT M^{RS} HOLTS,

Italian Ware House

at y^e two Olive Posts in y^e Broad part of the Strand almost
opposite to Exeter Change are Sold all Sorts of Italian Silks as

Lustrings, Sattins, Padesois, Velvets, Damasks,
&c.

Fans, Legorne Hats, Flowers Lute & Violin Strings,
Books of Essences, Venice Treacle, Balsomes,
&c.

And in a Back Ware house all Sorts of Italian
Wines, Florence Cordials, Oyl, Olives, Anchovies,
Capers, Vermicelli, Bolognia Saussidges, Par
-mesan Cheeses, Naple Soap,
&c.

XLIX

John Clark
LAMP LIGHTER
in Denmark Street, near St. Giles's Church, in the Feilds, furnisheth Gentlemen with all sorts of Globular Lamps, and Lights them by the Week, or Quarter, at ye Lowest Prices.

L

Wm Will: Conaway
near the Bull head in Dean-ſtreet
By Sʳ Anns Church.
Furniſheth Perſons of Quality & others
with Lamps, Lanthorns & Irons of all ſorts
Also keeps Servants to Light then
at Reaſonable rates.

A View of Francis Nobles Circulating Library.

Ravenet Scul

AT.

Francis Nobles

Large Circulating Library,

At

Otway's Head, in King Street, Covent Garden.

Books are

LENT to READ.

(Both English and French.)

At Half a Guinea a Year,

OR

Three Shillings a Quarter.

Note, New Books Bought as soon as Publish'd

Ready Money for any Library or Parcel of Books, or Books Exchang'd.

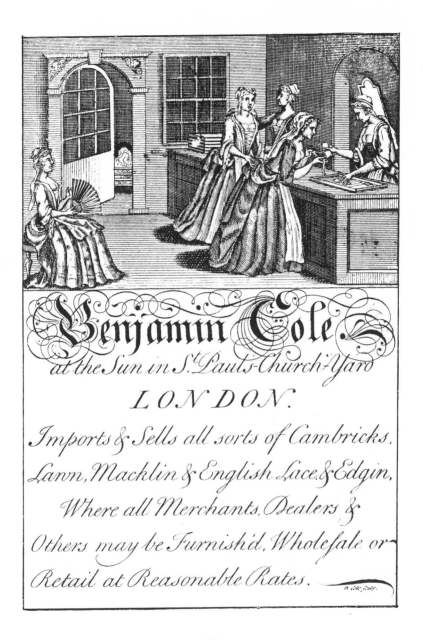

Benjamin Cole.

at the Sun in St Pauls-Church-Yard

LONDON.

Imports & Sells all sorts of Cambricks,

Lawn, Macklin & English Lace, & Edgin,

Where all Merchants, Dealers &

Others may be Furnish'd, Wholesale or

Retail at Reasonable Rates.

B Cole Sculp.

LIII

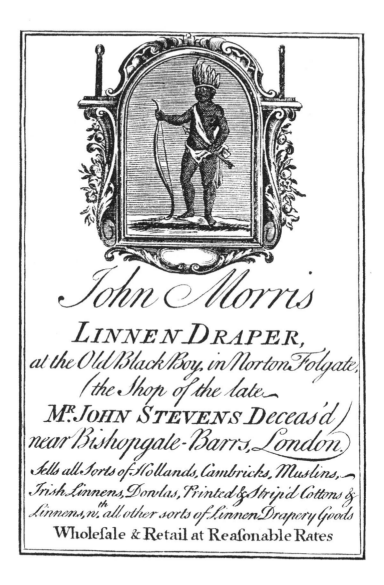

John Morris

LINNEN DRAPER,
at the Old Black Boy, in Norton Folgate,
the Shop of the late
M.ᴿ JOHN STEVENS Deceas'd
near Bishopgate-Barrs, London.

Sells all sorts of Hollands, Cambricks, Muslins,
Irish Linnens, Dowlas, Printed & Strip'd Cottons &
Linnens, w.ᵗʰ all other sorts of Linnen Drapery Goods

Wholesale & Retail at Reasonable Rates

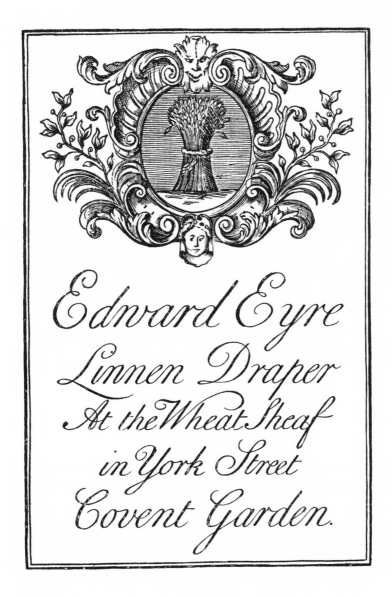

Edward Eyre
Linnen Draper
At the Wheat Sheaf
in York Street
Covent Garden.

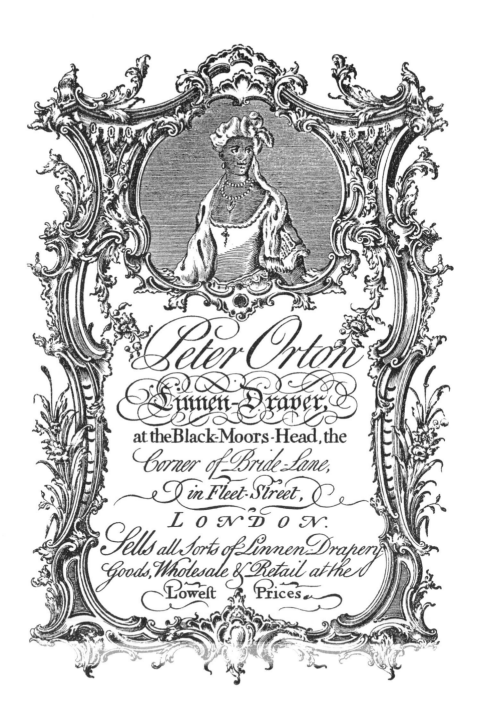

Peter Orton
Linnen-Draper,
at the Black-Moors-Head, the
Corner of Bride-Lane,
in Fleet-Street,
L O N D O N.
Sells all Sorts of Linnen Drapery
Goods, Wholesale & Retail at the
Lowest Prices

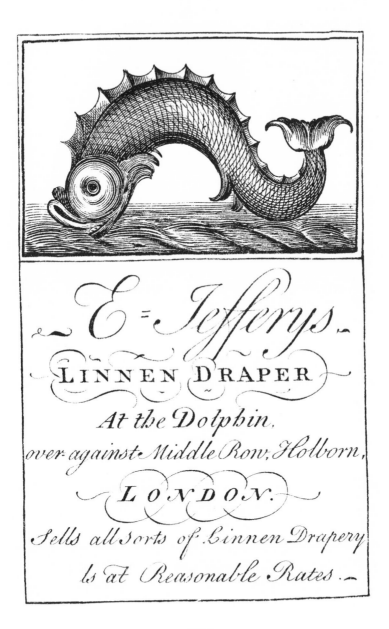

E. Jefferys

LINNEN DRAPER

At the Dolphin,
over against Middle Row, Holborn,

LONDON.

Sells all sorts of Linnen Drapery
ls at Reasonable Rates.

LVII

Edw: Nourse. Mercer

at y̅ᵉ Turks-Head, near Bow-Church, Cheapside,

LONDON.

Sells all Sorts of Genoa, Dutch, & English Velvets, Paduasoys of all Colours, Tabbys water'd or unwater'd, Rich Brocades, Damasks, & all Sorts of Flower'd Silks, Rich Florence & English Sattins, Figur'd & Stript Lutestrings, Ducapes, Mantuas, Sarsnets, & Persians. Likewise all Sorts of half Silks, as English, & Turkey Burdets, Cherry-derrys figur'd & Stript Donjars. Also all Sorts of Black Silks for Hoods, & Scarves, Worsted Damasks, Plodds, Superfine broad Camblets, Calimancoes, Camblitees, Black Russells, fine Callimancoes for Pettycoats and Yard wide Tammys or Stuffs. Likewise Short Cloaks, Manteels, Mantelets, & Velvet Hoods, ready made, with all other Sorts of Mercery Goods, Wholesale & Retail at y̅ᵉ lowest Prices

LVIII

Cranston

Mercer from Round Court

At the three Nuns & Wheatsheaf in Great Bridge Street

WESTMINSTER

Sells Variety of Silks and Stuffs

Viz.t

Sattins.	Persians.	Flower'd Mecklingbourgs.
Tabbies.	Fig.d & Plain Modes.	Masque.rade Venetians & plain Do.
Armozeens.	Thread Sattins.	Silk Camblets.
Ducapes.	Poplins.	Dorsetteens
Serge du Soys	Broglios.	Furni.re & other Stuff Damasks.
Mantuas.	Missinets.	Camblets. Russells. &
Sarcenets.	Lustrings.	Callimancoes.

Fig.d & Plain Yard wide Stuffs

Norwich Crapes of the most Fash.ble Mixtures

Bombazeens & other Goods for Mourning Lastings & double Callimancoes for Shoemakers
Cardinals, Cloaks, Hats, Bonnets, and Quilted Coats. Flannels & Bays

At the very lowest Rates.

LIX

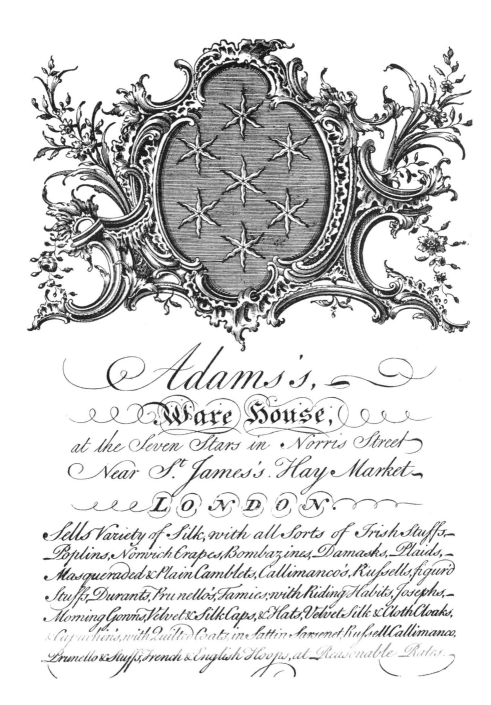

Adams's,

Ware House,

at the Seven Stars in Norris Street
Near S.t James's Hay Market
L O N D O N.

Sells Variety of Silk, with all Sorts of Irish Stuffs,
Poplins, Norwich Crapes, Bombazines, Damasks, Plaids,
Masqueraded & Plain Camblets, Callimanco's, Russells, figur'd
Stuffs, Durants, Prunello's, Tamies, with Riding Habits, Josephs,
Morning Gowns, Velvet & Silk Caps, & Hats, Velvet Silk & Cloth Cloaks,
& Capuchins, with Quilted Coats, in Sattin Sarsenet Russell Callimanco,
Prunello & Stuffs, French & English Hoops, at Reasonable Rates.

Wm Ryder & Edwd Nicklin
MERCERS,
at the Indian Queen by the Cloisters, West Smithfield,
LONDON.

Sell all Sorts of Rich Damasks, Broeaded Silks, Paduasoys, Tabbys, Sattins, Ducapes, Mantuas, Shagreens, Sergedusoys, Stript & Sprig'd Lutestrings, Dutch, Genoa & English Velvets, Black Silks, Bombazeens, Norwich Crapes, Poplins, Silk & Worsted Plads & Damasks, Broad & Narrow Camblets Calamancoes, Super fine Russels, with great Choice of Stuffs of every Sort: Hair Prunelloes & Princes Stuffs for Clergymen and Gentlemen of the Law

FINE CLOTHS AND DUFFINS,
Variety of Manteelets & Hoods, | Ladys Riding Habits &c.
Short Clokes & Long Scarves, | Mens Gowns & Banyans.
Quilted & Hoop Pettycoats. | Widows Weeds.

N.B. E. Nicklin, Remov'd from the Indian-King, Holborn.

Whitehead Rumball
(from Mr Boyds)
MERCER
at the Golden Anchor
near the New Church in
the Strand
LONDON.

Edward Argles

(From Goff & Kendall in the Borough)

at y.e Indian King (late M.r Nicklins) near Warwick Court Holborn,

London.

Sells Variety of MERCERY GOODS. Viz.:

Paduasoys, Damasks, Tabbys, Sattins, Ducapes, Armozeens, Dutch & Italian Mantuas, Stript Lutestrings, Genoa & Dutch Velvets, Shaggreens, Sergedusoys, Poplins, Irish Stuffs, Allopeens, Figurd Brolios, Incle Lutestrings, Burdetts, Norwich Crapes, Bombazeens, Black Silks, Hair Bines, Silk & Worsted Camblets, Worsted Damasks, Camblettees, Callimancoes, Plads and Stuffs of all Sorts.

Also Variety of Ready-made things. Viz.t

Short Cloaks, | *Gentlemens Morning Gowns,*
Velvet Hoods, Mantelets, | *Ladies Riding Habits.*

Quilted Coats and Hoops.

From ẏ Black Spread
Eagle in Shandoies
Street

GABRIEL DOVCE at ẏ Lamb &
Black Spread Eagle next door to the
Golden Goate in New Round Court
in ẏ Strand. Selleth all Sorts of
Silks Stuffs Norwich Crapes Cam=
=tells & all sorts of Black Silks for
Hoods & Scarves at Reasonable Rates

Garnham Edwards
At the Old Indian Queen

Faceing Hatton-Garden, Holborn.

Sells all sorts of Stuffs half Silks Nor-
wich Crapes Bombazeens, Irish Stuffs,
and Ducapes Allopeens, Black Silks, Per-
fians Brotios, Worsted Damasks, Camblets,
Callamancoes, Shaggreens Poplins Quilted Coats Ready made

Flanels, Bays Plads, and Short Cloaks.

LXV

Martha Wheatland, and Sister

MILLENERS, & HABERDASHERS,

At Queen Charlott's Head
Near Wood Street, Cheapside

London

Sell all sorts of Haberdashery & Fancy
Millenery Goods at the Lowest Prices.
NB. Great Variety of Italian Flowers
And Egrets,
With Necklaces, and Ear-rings
in the moſt Elegant Taſte.

J. W. Tringham Sculp.   Castle Alley Royal Exchan.

LXVI

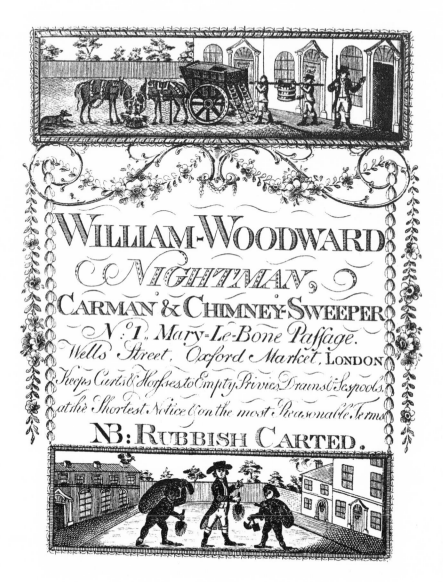

WILLIAM-WOODWARD
NIGHTMAN,
CARMAN & CHIMNEY-SWEEPER
N.º 1, Mary-Le-Bone Passage.
Wells Street, Oxford Market, LONDON
Keeps Carts & Horses to Empty Privies, Drains & Sespools,
at the Shortest Notice & on the most Reasonable Terms
NB: RUBBISH CARTED.

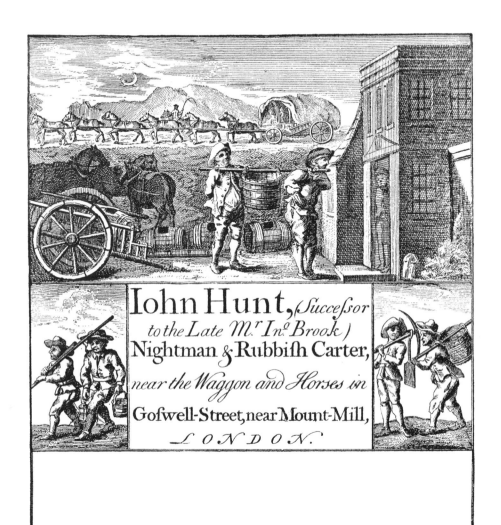

John Hunt, (Successor to the Late M.ʳ In.º Brook) Nightman & Rubbish Carter, near the Waggon and Horses in Gofwell-Street, near Mount-Mill, LONDON.

At James Wheeleys Paper Hanging Warehouse
Opposite the Church in little Britain, LONDON.
Are Manufactor'd & Sold all Sorts of Emboss'd Chints & Common Papers for
Rooms, with great variety of Papier Machee, & other Ornaments for Cielings,
Halls, Stair Cases &c. N.B. All kind of Furniture are exactly
Match'd and compleatly put up.

LXIX

THE
Manufactory for PaperHangings,
Painted or Printed from Copper Plates or Wood,
By MATT.ˢ DARLY.
Painter, Engraver, & Paper Stainer,
Wholesale & Retail at the Lowest Prices,
At the Acorn facing Hungerford, STRAND
Cielings, Pannels, Staircases, Chimney
Boards, &c Neatly fitted up either with
Paintings or Stainings, in the
Modern, Gothic or Chinese Tastes
for Town or Country;
& large Allowance for Ready Money.
NB. Paper for Exportation
And Sketches, Or
Designs for Gentlemen's
Different Fancies.
Letters Post paid Duly Answerd

Engraving in all its Branches,
Viz. Visiting Tickets, Coats of Arms,
Seals, Book Plates, Frontispieces,
Shopkeepers Bills &c
In greater Variety & Cheaper than
at any other Shop in Town.

LXX

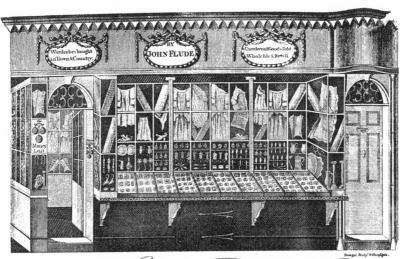

John Flude

PAWNBROKER and **SILVERSMITH**

N.º 2 Grace Church Street

London.

Lends Money on Plate, Watches, Jewells, Wearing Apparel, Houshold Goods, & Stock in Trade.

NB

Goods Sent from any Part of y Country directed as above, shall be duly attended too & the Utmost Value lent thereon.

LXXI

Now the gentle GALES
Faning their Odoriferous Wings, Dispense

Native Perfumes; & whisper whence they stole
Those balmy SPOILS.

THE STORAX AND ROSE — THE MYRRH AND FRANKINCENSE

In Adoration to the God of Day
Rich Sweet Perfumes the Eastern Princes Pay ⸺

In Jewish Temples Spread the Fragrant Scent,
And Christian Churches where the Knees are bent.

Richard Warren PERFUMER

at the Golden Fleece in Mary le Bonne Street Golden Square, & fronting Wood Street, Cheapside

London.

Imports, Makes & Sells

All Sorts of the Richest Perfumery Goods in all its branches & greatest perfection, Wholesale, Retail & for Export.

LXXII

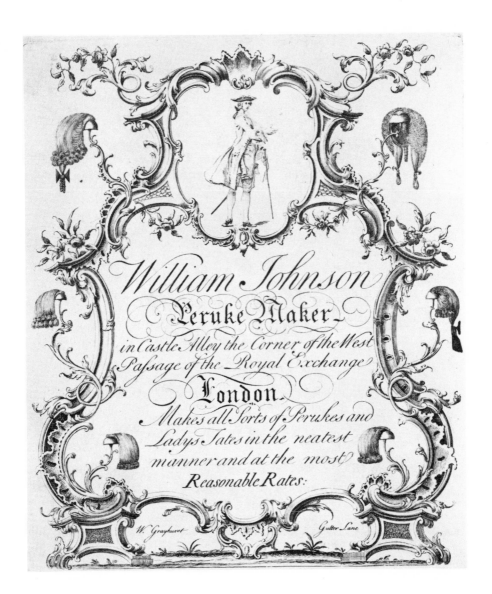

William Johnson
Peruke Maker
in Castle Alley the Corner of the West
Passage of the Royal Exchange
London
Makes all Sorts of Perukes and
Ladys Tates in the neatest
manner and at the most
Reasonable Rates.

W. Grayhurst   Gutter Lane

LXXIII

Thomas Gibbons,
Peruke Maker,
at the Blew & White Peruke,
in Rosemary Lane,

LONDON.

Makes and Sells all sorts of Perukes
Wholesale & Retale, at Reasonable Rates.
NB. the best of left Off Wiggs, Sold Wholesale & Retale

Tho.̱ Scattergood
PEWTERER
at the Blackmoors head near the
South Sea House in Bishops-
gate street LONDON
Makes & Sells all sorts of Pewter.
Wholesale & Retail
at reasonable Rates

LXXV

John Kenrick

Working-Pewterer,

at His Warehouse

near Cherry-Garden Stairs,

ROTHERHITH.

Makes Superfine White hard Metal
Dishes & Plates & all other Sorts of
Pewter Wares in a curious manner.
Where all Merchants and others,
may be supply'd Wholesale or Retail
at Reasonable Rates.

LXXVI

On London Bridge

LXXVII

Dorothy Mercier
Printseller, and Stationer,
at the Golden Ball,
in Wind-mill Street, facing Silver Street, Golden Square,
London.

Sells all Sorts of Italian, French, and Flemish Prints.
Buys & Sells all manner of Old Prints.
Likewise Frames Prints, in the Neatest & Genteelest Taste.
Where may be had all Sorts of Paper for Drawing, &c.
The best Black Lead Pencils, Black, Red & White Chalk.
Variety of Water-Colours, and Camels Hair Pencils.
The best Dutch Sealing Wax
Sells Flower Pieces, in Water-Colours, Painted by her self, from the Life.
And Fanns for Ladies, in a New & Elegant manner.
Also all sorts of Shop Books, Finest Writing Paper Both Gilt, & plain, in all sizes
English, Dutch, & French Drawing Paper, Abortive Vellum, for Drawing,
Writing Vellum, the Silk Paper for Drawing, with Different Sizes of
Message Paper, & Message Cards, Fine Black, Brown, & Blue India Ink.

LXXVIII

Dr James's Powder for

FEVERS,

And other Inflammatory Distempers,

Publish'd by Virtue of

His Majesty's Royal Letters Patent;

WILL remove (as has been Experienced in many thousand Cases) any continual Acute *Fever* in a few Hours, though attended with Convulsions Light-headedness, and the worst Symptoms: But if taken in the Beginning of a Fever, *one Dose* is generally sufficient to perform a Cure.

These POWDERS are Sold only by J. NEWBERY, at

The Bible and Sun in S.t Pauls Church Yard, over against the North-Door of the Church, at 2.s 6.d the two Doses; with good Allowance to those who buy them for Charitable Uses or to Sell again.

LXXIX

Henry Patten
RAZOR-MAKER,
at the Saw and Crown,
in Middle Row Holborn,
LONDON.
Makes all sorts of the Best & Newest
Fashion Razors, Scissors, Lancets, Penknives,
Pocket Knives, Table Knives & Forks, Also
Mounts the Best Blades, in Silver, Ivory, or
Agate Hafts, &c. Likewise the Best Fleames, and
Horse Scissors, and all manner of Cutlery Ware,
Made in the Best Manner,
at Reasonable Rates.
N.B. The above Instruments Carefully Ground & Set

Silver Spurs, Buckles, Buttons &c.   E. Warner, Sculp.

LXXX

Cupping Instruments Made and Mended —

James Bernardeau,
Razor Maker, at the Pistol & L in
Russell Court, in Drury Lane.
Make & Sell Razors, Sizzors, Penknives,
Lancetts, and all other Instruments.
Also Silver, Chiney, Ivory, Ebeny, Handled Knives & Forks &c.

JAQUES BERNARDEAU,
Couteliee a Lenseigne du Pistolet et L dans Rus
sell Court, dans Drury Lane.
Fait et Vend Razoirs, Ciseaux, Ganifes,
Lancetts et tout autre Instruments.
Vieux Razoirs et Lancetts Emoulu et passe avec Soins.

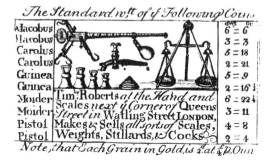

LXXXII

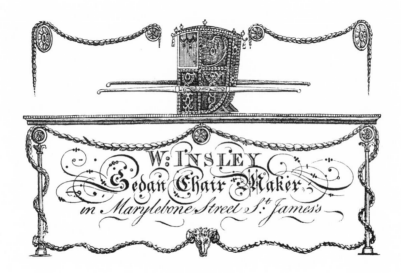

LXXXIII

TERMS of Mrs MASQUERIER'S
Boarding School,
Upper End of Church Lane,
K E N S I N G T O N.

Board including French, English, Writing, Arithmetic, Geography, Needle-
work, & Dancing, for Twenty Guineas a Year, and One Guinea Entrance.
Parents or Guardians
may depend on the utmost care taken of the Young Ladies morals and
manners, and a particular tenderness shewn to their persons.

NB: The house is genteel
and the situation
remarkably
healthful.

To those who do not chuse
to learn all the above
branches, a reasonable
deduction will be
made.

A Shilling Stage to Holborn, Wood-Street, & the Bank several times a Day.

LXXXIV

William Lem
BROKER,
Sells Ships or parts of Ships by Publick
or private Sale; Lets Ships to Freight;
Enters & Clears Ships at the Custom House;
Makes Insurances on Ships & Merchandize;
Attends at his Office in Exchange Alley, LONDON
From 9 in the Morning, till 8 in the Evening.
Orders left at his House in Lime Street,
or at his OFFICE,
will be punctually comply'd with.

J. Kirk Sc. St Pauls

LXXXV

John Snowdon
Shoe-Maker
at the Angel & Three Shoes, in Cranboum Alley,
near Leicester Fields,
London
Makes & Sells all sorts of Shoes, Boots,
Pumps, & Slippers, & Cloggs &c Wholesale
or Retail, at Reasonable Rates.

LXXXVI

DANIEL RICHARDS
STATIONER
At S.ᵗ Andrews-Church Holborn
LONDON!
Makes & Sells Paper Books of all Sizes, for Merchants or Tradesmen; Viz. Shop-Books, Pockett-Books, Cyphering-Books, Coppybooks, Slates, Slate Pens, Stampt Paper & Parchment, & all Sorts of Paper for Grocers, and Chandlers, & all other Stationery Wares, Whole sale & Retail at y Lowest Prices.

LXXXVII

Charles Peter. Surgeon *Served* King Charles $\check{y}$ 2^{d} *in $\check{y}$ Dutch*
warrs. Surgeon *of $\check{y}$ Horse guards* to King James *and* Surgeon *of the*
Housbold to King William *daily prepares his* Cordial Tincture &
Pills *which have cured Thousands of $\check{y}$* Collick, Stone, Gravell;

lived between 30 & 40 *Years.* Laus Deo. 1705. Ætat. 57.

Ant. Schoonian pinx.   Jos. Nutting Sculp

ECCE·AGNUS DEI·QUI·TOLLIT PECCATA·MUNDI

Stent feat *Gutter Lane*

Thomas Payne

TALLOW CHANDLER

in S.ᵗ Anns Lane near Aldersgate

𝕷𝖔𝖓𝖉𝖔𝖓

Makes and Sells all Sorts of

Fine Mould & Store Candles

Also the fine and true Sperma Cœti Candles

Wholesale and Retail.

LXXXIX

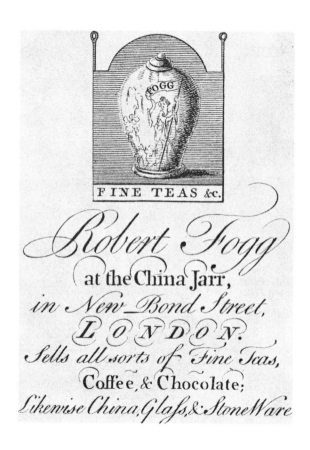

FINE TEAS &c.

Robert Fogg
at the China Jarr,
in New Bond Street,
LONDON.
Sells all sorts of Fine Teas,
Coffee, & Chocolate;
Likewise China, Glass, & StoneWare

Robert Howard

Tin-plate-worker *and* Brazier,
at the Wheatsheaf and Trumpet,
SMITHFIELD BARS, LONDON.

Makes & Sells all Sorts of Tin wares
and Brasiery, Wholesale & Retail.
Likewise Sells the best Hard Metal Pewter-
Dishes & Plates, Alehouse Pots, & Wine Mea-
sures, Tea-pots; Pewter, Occumy & White Metal
Spoons, Bellows, Box-irons, & Flat-irons. All
Sorts of Candlesticks & Snuffers. Japand Plate-
warmers & Coal-scoops, Iron-sifters & Dust Shovels,
& Fine Spermacæti Oil.

Kitchen Vessels —— Tind & Mended.

The best Price for Old Metal.

XCI

INDUSTRY. INDOLENCE

Samuel Forsaith
TRUNKMAKER,
At Industry and Indolence, in Long Acre,
London

Late Apprentice to Mʳ Smith, Trunkmaker to his Majesty
Makes & Sells all sorts of Campaign, and strong Iron bound
Trunks for travelling in foreign Roads, Sumpter & Portmanteau
Trunks, Budgets & Trunks for Post Chaises, Cover'd Hampers,
Canvas and Leather Valeeses for Bedding, Leather Portmanteaus,
Saddle Bags, Fire Buckets, Jacks, Powder Flasks, Harvest
Bottles, Peruke Boxes, travelling Writing desks; Cases for
Plate, China, Glasses, & Musical Instruments. With all other
Sorts of Trunkmakers Goods.

Gentlemen Merchants, and Shopkeepers, in Town or Country, may be well supplied with
all Sorts of Packing Trunks, and Hair & Gilt Nests of Trunks for Exportation, &c,

NB. Noblemen, Gentlemen, and others, who shall please to Favour me with their
Orders for any of the abovementioned Commodities, may depend on being dealt
with for a very moderate Profit, and the Lowest Prices fixed without abatement,
and the Goods warranted as neat and substantial as any in LONDON.

John Clements
Trunk-Maker.
at the Old Original Shop the Corner
of St Pauls, next Cheapside, LONDON.
Makes & Sells all sorts of Campaign Post
Chaise, Portmantua Trunks, and Leather
Portmantuas, Leather Baggs, Cloth Cloak
Baggs, Plate Cases, Perrivigg Boxes, Gilded nest
of Trunks, Fire Buckets, Vallees for Beding,
Canteens and all Sorts of other Leather Ware.
Wholesale & Retail, at Reasonable Rates.
NB. Kitchen Hampers & Ponder Baggs.

STEEL SPRING TRUSSES

and other Instruments
to help the Weak & Lame ,

BY

John Richardson

at the Golden Key,

Prescot Street, Goodmans Fields,

——— LONDON. ———

Elizabeth Barton Stent Daughter &
Successor to the late Robert Stent

Eliz Barton Stent
At the Turners Arms in
Little Britain

Makes & sells Baggamon Tables & Draft
boards & Table-men, Draft men of all sorts &
sizes, Chesmen & Dice-boxes & Dice, Orrange
& Orriss peas for Issues & Ruff Orranges,
Ivory Syrrenges, Syrrenge staves for Pen ter
Syrrenges, & Syrrenge pipes, box & bone, Clyster
pipes, horse Clyster pipes, Curtain Rings Ivory
Thimbles & Needle Cases, Ivory Pounce Boxes,
Ivory-folders & folding-knives, Lignum Vitæ
and Ivory Shavings.
Wholesale & Retale at reasonable Rates .

XCV

George Smithson

Broker Undertaker & Sworn Appraiſer,

Oppoſite the Bull and Gate, Holbourn

LONDON.

Buys & Sells all sorts of Household Goods,

&c. at Reasonable Rates

NB. Funerals Perform'd.

Robert Green

Coffin Maker & Undertaker,

at the four Coffins S.t Margaret's Hill;

Southwark

Sells and Lets all Manner of Furniture for
Funerals, on Reasonable Terms.

VIZ.t

Velvet Palls, Hangings for Rooms, large Silver'd
Candlesticks & Sconces, Tapers & Wax Lights, Heraldry,
Feathers & Velvets, fine Cloth Cloaks & midling D.o Rich
Silk Scarves, Allamode & Sarsnett Hatbands, Italian Crape
by the Piece or Hatband, black & white Favours, Cloth Black
or Grey Bays & Flannel D.o Burying Crapes of all Sorts,
fine Quilting & Quilted Mattrices the best Laced, Plain &
Shammy Gloves, Kidd & Lamb D.o &c. N.B All Sorts of Plates &
Handles for Coffins in Brass, Lead or Tin, likewise Nails of all Sorts
Coffins & Shrouds of all Sizes ready made. Where Country Chapmen
and others may be Furnish'd   in the most Expeditious
Manner, on the   least Notice

THE
ROYAL BED AND STAR

James Rodwell

Upholster and Sworn Appraiser.

*At the Royal Bed & Star, the 2.ᵈ Door from the Corner
of New Broad Street, faceing Bedlam Walk in Moorfields.*

LONDON.

*Buys, Sells & Appraises all manner of Household Goods, New & Old, as Standing
Beds & Bedding, Chests of Drawers, Desk & Book-Cases, Bueroe Desks, Card,
Dining, Breakfast & Dressing Tables, (in Mahogeny, Walnut tree or Wainscot) Chairs
of all sorts, Settee & Bueroe Bedsteads, Sconces, Pier, Chimney & Dressing Glasses
with all other sorts of Upholstery, Cabinet & Braizery Goods &c.*

XCVIII

Robert Legg

Upholder, Appraiser & Undertaker,

at the sign of y.ᵉ Leg near Southampton Street, in

Holborn

Son of the late Rob.ᵗ Legg

opposite Bloomsbury Market.

Darly Sculp. Chandos Street.

XCIX

Peter Hodgson
Woollen-Draper,
At the Wool Pack
in Grace-Church Street
LONDON.
Sells all Sorts of Broad
Cloths, German Serges &
Shalloons.
Wholesale & Retail

C

Rich.ᵈ Fanson,
Woollen-Draper,
at the Golden Fleece,
The North side of St. Pauls Church Yard,
L O N D O N.
Sells all sorts of Woollen Drapery Goods,
Wholesale & Retail, at the Lowest Prices.

J. Kirk Sculp.   St. Pauls Church Yard.

CI

INDEX

NOTE.—The reader should also consult the separate right-hand lists in Chapters IV and VI, pp. 22-25 and 38-62. The roman numerals (caps.) refer to the Plate numbers.